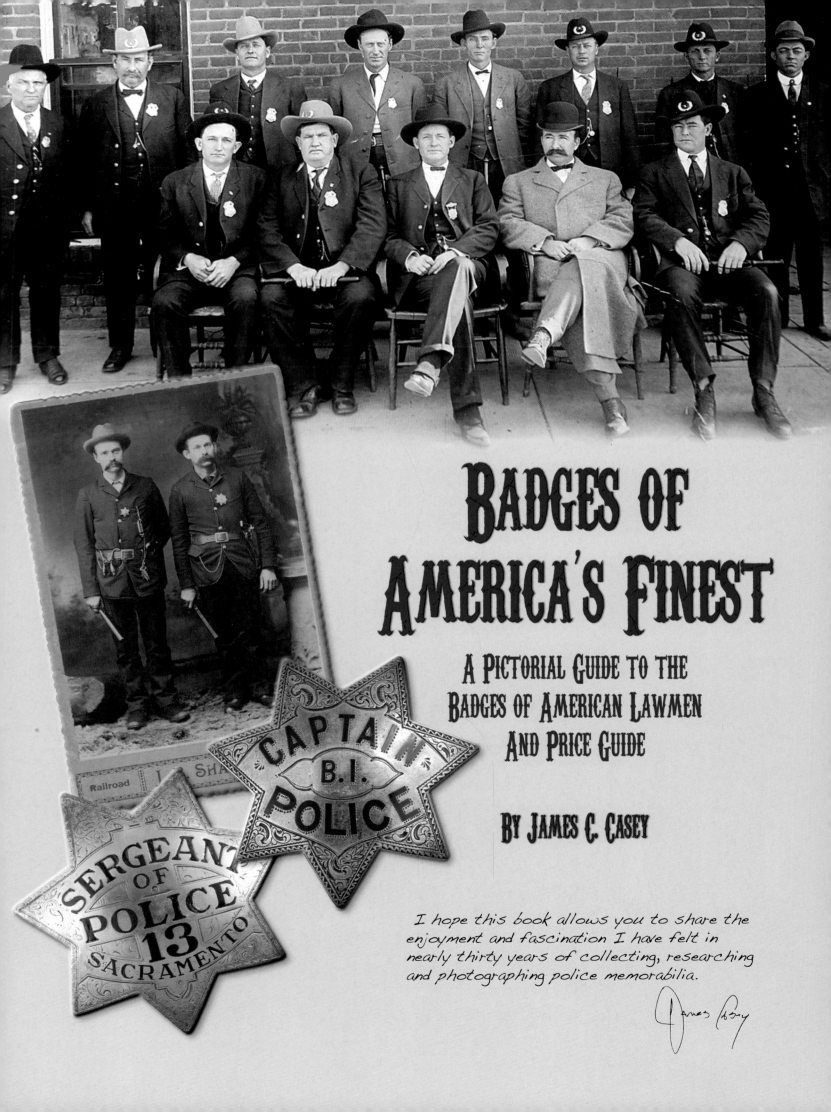

Badges of America's Finest

A Pictorial Guide to the Badges of American Lawmen And Price Guide

By James C. Casey

I hope this book allows you to share the enjoyment and fascination I have felt in nearly thirty years of collecting, researching and photographing police memorabilia.

James Casey

M.T. Publishing Company, Inc.
P.O. Box 6802
Evansville, Indiana 47719-6802
www.mtpublishing.com

Copyright © 2008
James C. Casey

Graphic Designer: Elizabeth A. Dennis

Library of Congress
Control Number 2008925493

Printed in the United States
of America

ISBN: 978-1-932439-51-9

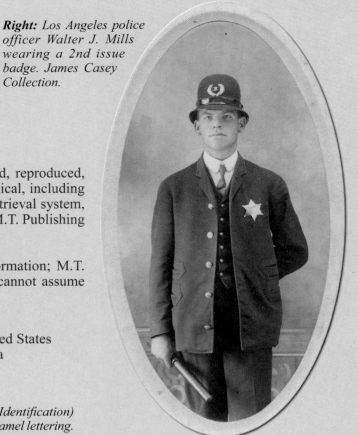

Right: Los Angeles police officer Walter J. Mills wearing a 2nd issue badge. James Casey Collection.

Preceding page: (Top right badge) Captain Max Fisher's B. I. (Bureau of Identification) sterling silver star, circa 1900, made of sterling silver with hard fired blue enamel lettering. Each letter has hand engraved shadowing. Captain Fisher was considered a high authority on identification matters and was rated in "Police World" as one of the four great men in America versed in the science of visual identification. California's present CII (criminal identification and information) owes its existence mainly to the efforts put forth by Captain Fisher at sessions of the State Legislature. James Casey Collection. Value D (Bottom left badge) Above: Sergeant of Police #13 Sacramento, sterling silver, hand engraved. Made by Ed Jones Oakland, California, circa 1935. Bob Davis Collection. Value B

Below: Buck Garrett Chief of Police, with Ardmore, I. T. (Indian Territory) Police Department, circa 1905. Photograph by Webb. James Casey Collection.

Contents

Above: San Luis Obispo, California, police officer wearing 1st issue badge #3. Photo by Arnold. James Casey Collection.

Below left: Sausalito Police badge #6, nickel silver with Carnival lettering. James Casey Photograph. Value A

Above: Cabinet photo of a Philadelphia House Sergeant. Photo by Dgan & Holloway. James Casey Collection.

INTRODUCTION

On May 27, 1845 *The Philadelphia Ledger* and *Daily Transcript* reported that the day policemen of that city had begun to wear a badge designating them as the City Police. This is the earliest record describing the issuance of a metal police badge in the United States that I am aware of. However Philadelphia had a day night police patrol going back to 1830. Prior to 1830 the city had only a night watch directed by the Constable of each ward.

The City of New York was soon to issue metal police badges to their newly formed police department in July of 1845. Baltimore did likewise on October 20, 1851 and Boston on April 30, 1853. By this time most of the large city police departments in the U.S. were wearing badges of various design and size. The following pages will explore the badges of America's Finest. From the very plain to the jewelers' art of hand engraving on sterling and gold the American police badge is highly prized by collectors.

As a basic guide to interested readers you will notice that many of the badges pictured have a caption ending with a capital letter that corresponds to the price guide below. Please keep in mind that this is a basic and general price guide intended to give a ballpark value of various types of badges. As in all collectibles and antiques, condition and rarity can greatly affect the value.

A less than $1,000
B $1,000 to $2,000
C $2,000 to $5,000
D $5,000 to $10,000
E over $10,000

Rare interior image of a sheriff's office. James Casey Collection.

5

ALASKA

Above: *1st issue Alaska Highway Patrol #37, made of nickel silver. James Casey Photograph. Value B*

Right: *Fish, Game Ranger from the Yukon Delta Refuge, made of nickel. James Casey Photo Collection. Value A*

Above: *City of Nome. This Nome Alaska eagle top shield has hard fired blue enamel. Doug Gist Collection. Value A*

Right: *North Pole, Alaska. This unique design features a six point star surrounded by a wreath and surmounted by an eagle with wings spread. Doug Gist Collection. Value A*

ARIZONA

Left: *Yuma Arizona Police, gold colored with hard fired blue enamel. James Casey Photo Collection. Value A*

Above front and back: *Chief Tucson Arizona Police, D. J. Hays, This gold plated Chiefs badge features hard fired blue enamel and is named on the front. Doug Gist Collection. Value A*

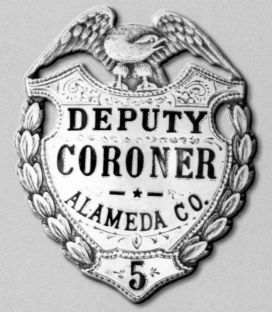

Left: Alameda County, California dual titled badge. Presentation reads: "Presented To Cletus I. Howell by Members of Berkeley Police Dept Feb 1928 Irvine & Jachens 14K." Private Collection. James Casey Photograph. Value D

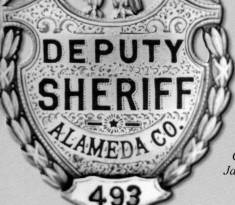

Above: Deputy Coroner Alameda County #5 done in sterling silver with hard fired black enamel and hand engraving, circa 1950. Badges from the Coroner's office are somewhat scarce. Made by Ed Jones Co. Oakland, California. James Casey Photo Collection. Value A

Left: Deputy Sheriff Alameda County, California #493. A beautiful Ed Jones Company design with a gold front. James Casey Photograph. Value A

CALIFORNIA

Above: Henry N. Morse, Sheriff, Alameda County, gun belt and buckle belonging to Sheriff Harry Morse, a famous California lawman. John Boessenecker Collection

Above: Oakland SPCA #31 Officer Alameda County. This unique and rare badge was made by the Morton Jewelry Company, Oakland, California. The enamel and engraving looked to be the work of George Fake and research revealed that he indeed went to work for Morton Jewelry after closing his own business. James Casey Photo Collection. Value B

7

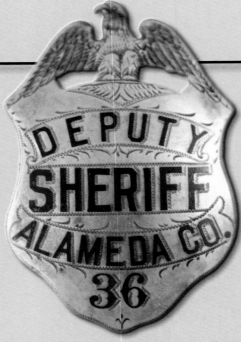

Above: Deputy Sheriff Alameda County California, #36, sterling silver eagle top shield with hard fired blue enamel, hand engraved, 3", circa 1925. James Casey Photograph. Value C

Above: Deputy Sheriff Alameda County California, #77, sterling silver eagle top shield with hard fired blue enamel, hand engraved, 3", circa 1940. James Casey Photograph. Value C

Above: Deputy Sheriff Alameda County California, sterling silver eagle top shield with hard fired blue enamel, two syles of lettering, hand engraved, 3", circa 1930. James Casey Photograph. Value C

Right: Deputy Sheriff Alameda County California 3" sterling silver eagle top shield with unique enameled engraving. Made by Jeweler Geo. Fake Oakland, California, circa 1900. James Casey Photograph. Value C

Above front and back: Deputy Sheriff Alameda County California sterling silver eagle top shield with unique enameled engraving, 3". Made by Jeweler Geo. Fake Oakland, California, circa 1890, T-pin. James Casey Photograph. Value C

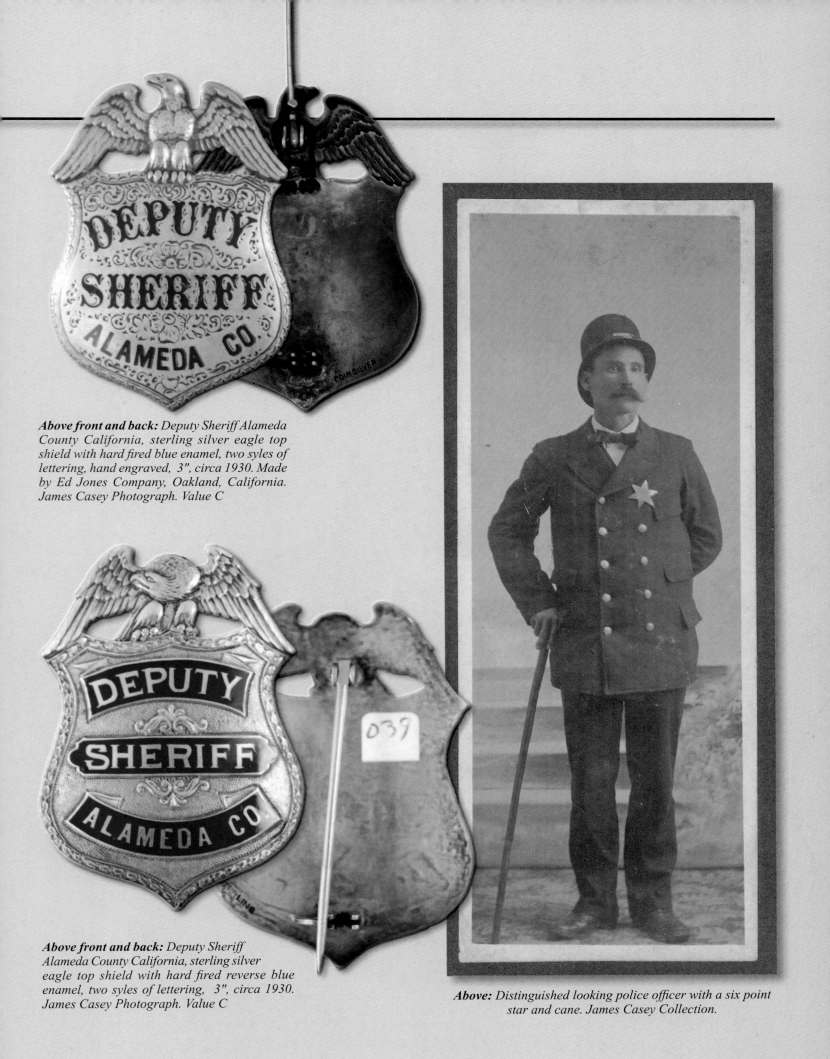

Above front and back: Deputy Sheriff Alameda County California, sterling silver eagle top shield with hard fired blue enamel, two syles of lettering, hand engraved, 3", circa 1930. Made by Ed Jones Company, Oakland, California. James Casey Photograph. Value C

Above front and back: Deputy Sheriff Alameda County California, sterling silver eagle top shield with hard fired reverse blue enamel, two syles of lettering, 3", circa 1930. James Casey Photograph. Value C

Above: Distinguished looking police officer with a six point star and cane. James Casey Collection.

9

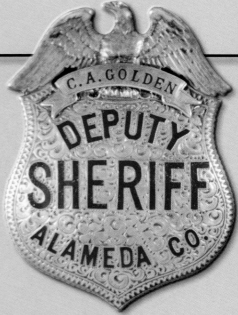

Above: Deputy Sheriff Alameda County done in sterling silver with hard fired blue enamel and hand engraving, circa 1940. Made by Ed Jones Company, Oakland, California. James Casey Photo Collection. Value A

Above: Deputy Sheriff Alameda County California named badge, "C. A. Golden." Sterling silver, hard fired blue enamel, hand engraved, circa 1920. Made by Ed Jones Company Oakland, California. James Casey Photograph. Value C

Above: Deputy Sheriff Alameda County #4T. A gold colored badge with hard fired blue enamel, circa 1950. Made by Ed Jones Company, Oakland, California. James Casey Photo Collection. Value A

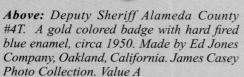

Left: Emeryville 8 Police - A silver color 7 point star with hard fired black enamel lettering. Old style from this smaller Alameda County city located right on the bay. Patina is abundant on this old timer. Hallmarked: Ed Jones & Co., Oakland, Cal. Sterling. Photograph by Godfrey Gigiorgi. Al Mize Collection. Value A

Above: Oakland, California, police officer wearing badge #12, circa 1900. James Casey Collection.

Above: Deputy Sheriff Alameda County California sterling silver eagle top shield, hand engraved, Hallmark: Ed Jones Company Oakland, California, Sterling used in 1900-1920 era. Photograph by Godfrey Gigiorgi. Al Mize Collection. Value B

Far left and left: Hard to find set from Alpine County, California. Sheriff, 3" eagle top shield, nickel silver, circa 1930. Deputy Sheriff circa 1940 2 1/2" nickel silver. Authentic badges from Alpine Company are very difficult to find. Value C and B.

Above: Constable Alviso Cal Marshal. Nickel silver, soft black enamel. Rick Sprain Collection. Value A

Left: Constable Alviso, California. circa 1900, made of nickel silver. James Casey Photograph. Value A

Above: Constable Alviso Township. Nickel silver with soft black enamel, circa 1940. Rick Sprain Collection. Value A

Right: Attractive Chief of Police badge in sterling silver and hard fired blue enamel with a 10 karat gold center star adorned with a ruby. Worn by Chief Bacigalupi in Alviso, California, which went defunct around 1964 and was absorbed by the City of San Jose, California. James Casey Photograph. Value C

11

Left: Amador County. Deputy Sheriff, made by the Ed Jones Company, Oakland, California. Nickel silver, circa 1940. James Casey Photo Collection. Value A

Left: City Marshal, Banning, California - A silver color eagle top shield with soft black enamel lettering and a saddle pin back. Used in 1900-1920 era. No Hallmark. Photograph by Godfrey Gigiorgi. Al Mize Collection. Value A

Above: City of Avalon #33 Police, nickel silver, circa 1935, James Casey Photograph. Value B

Above: Bayshore, California #3 Police, nickel silver, made by Irvine & Jachens, circa 1930, James Casey Photograph. Value A

Above: City Marshal Benicia, California Sterling silver with hard fired black enamel, with T-pin, circa 1890. James Casey Photo Collection. Value C

Above: *Deputy Sheriff Butte County - A silver color circle with cut out 5 point star and soft black enamel lettering. A beautiful and unique badge from the old west. Photograph by Godfrey Digiorgi. Hallmark: Ed Jones, Oakland, California. Al Mize Collection. Value A*

Right front and back: *Undersheriff Butte County California sterling silver badge worn by "James R. Evans" who later became Chief of Police in Chico, California. Points have die struck design, hard fired blue enamel. Made by Ed Jones Co. Oakland, California. James Casey Photograph. Value C*

Above: *Under Sheriff Butte County California made by Ed Jones Company, Oakland, California, circa 1960. James Casey Photo Collection. Value A*

Left: *Gridley California Police, made of nickel silver, circa 1940. James Casey Photo Collection. Value A*

Above: *Deputy Sheriff of Calaveras County, California, eagle top shield, nickel silver, circa 1910, 2½". James Casey Photograph. Value B*

Left: Police 15 Chico, nickel, solf black enamel, circa 1930, made by Ed Jones Company Oakland, California. James Casey Photograph. Value A

Above: Chico Police Department #52 Traffic Supervisor, circa 1950. James Casey Photo Collection. Value A

Above: Detective #8 Police from Chico, California. Sterling silver, hard fired black enamel, hand engraved, 3½", circa 1870. Jeweler made. James Casey Collection. Value D

Above: Unknown Imperial County, California, lawman working with Walter Mills. James Casey Collection.

14

Above and right front and back:
Sheriff C.D. Stanton, Colusa County,
California. Gold wash over nickel silver,
made by Moise-K Company San Francisco.
Sheriff Stanton served from 1907-1925.
James Casey Photograph. Value B

Right: *Martinez 2 Police - A silver color seven*
point star with hard fired black enamel lettering.
Hand engraving and hand chasing make this
badge a beauty of the historic past. An oldie from
this city that is the county seat of Contra
Costa County. Used in 1930-1938 era.
Hallmark: Ed Jones & Co., Oakland,
Cal. STERLING Photograph by Godfrey
Gigiorgi. Al Mize Collection. Value B

Above: *Colusa County # 064 Deputy*
Sheriff, made of nickel silver, circa 1940,
James Casey Photo Collection. Value A

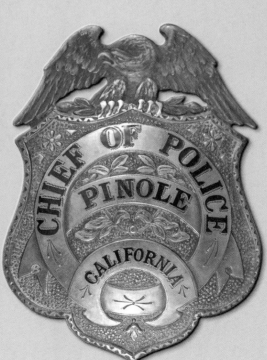

Right: *Richmond*
California #8 Lieutenant
Police, sterling silver, hand
engraved, hard fired black
enamel, made by the Ed Jones
Company, Oakland, California,
circa 1960. James Casey
Photo Collection. Value A

Above: *Chief of Police, Pinole, California*
in Contra Costa County. Sterling silver with
hard fired blue enamel. Private Collection.
James Casey Photograph. Value C

CALIFORNIA

Right: Del Norte County Deputy Sheriff, a nickel shield made by Moise-K San Francisco, California, circa 1925. James Casey Photo Collection. Value A

Right: Sheriff, Del Norte County, Austin "Bud" Huffman, gold front with hard fired blue enamel, made by Ed Jones Oakland, California. James Casey Photo Collection. Value B

Right: Undersheriff Del Norte County, California, circa 1950, James Casey Photo Collection. Value A

Right: Constable Klamath, Del Norte County, made of nickel silver, circa 1945. James Casey Photo Collection. Value A

Above right: Chief Crescent City Police. This chiefs badge was worn by Dan Nations. Doug Gist Collection. Value A

Right: Chief of Police Dan Nations wearing his Crescent City, California badge. Doug Gist Collection.

Above right: Matron Del Norte County #3, circa 1950, James Casey Collection. Value A

Above: Chief Civil Deputy, circa 1950, James Casey Collection. Value A

Above right: Chief Criminal Deputy, circa 1950, James Casey Collection. Value A

Right: This image features a badge that any collector would enjoy seeing in person. James Casey Collection.

17

Above: Gold front, hard fired blue enamel, hand engraved, circa 1960. Keith Bushey Collection. Value B

Above: Sterling silver, hard fired blue enamel, hand engraved, circa 1899. James Casey Photo Collection. Value D

Left: Sterling silver, hard fired blue enamel, circa 1944, James Casey Photo Collection. Value A

Above: Deputy Sheriff Fresno County, circa 1900, made by Fresno Stamp & Stationary. James Casey Photo Collection. Value A

Above: Deputy Constable Fresno California. Sterling silver Fresno deputy constable badge, circa 1890s, inscribed on reverse, W.P. Lyon." W. Parker Lyon (1865-1949) was the pioneer western collector and owner of the huge Pony Express Museum near Los Angeles."John Boessenecker Collection. Value B

18

Left: *Constable Garberville Judicial District Humboldt County - Silver color shield with soft black enamel lettering and saddle pin back. Old timer from yesteryear. Photograph by Godfrey Gigiorgi. Al Mize Collection. Value A*

Left: *Wm. Pederson, Sheriff Humboldt County, California. 14k layered gold adorned with four rubies. Hard fired blue enamel. Private Collection. James Casey Photograph. Value D*

Above right: *Fortuna, Humboldt County, California, circa 1950, made of nickel. James Casey Photo Collection. Value A*

Right: *Constable Table Bluff Township, from Humboldt County California, sterling silver, hard fired blue enamel. James Casey Photo Collection. Value B*

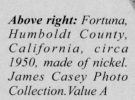

Above: *Nice old nickel Deputy Sheriff, Humboldt County, circa 1920. James Casey Photo Collection. Value A*

Left: *T.M. Brown Sheriff, Humboldt County, sterling silver, hard fired black enamel. T. M. Brown was the last Sheriff of Klamath County California before being elected sheriff of the newly reorganized county of Humboldt which included parts of the old Klamath County. Klamath County bears the unenviable distinction of being the only county in California that completely disappeared. It was dissolved March 28, 1874. Value C*

19

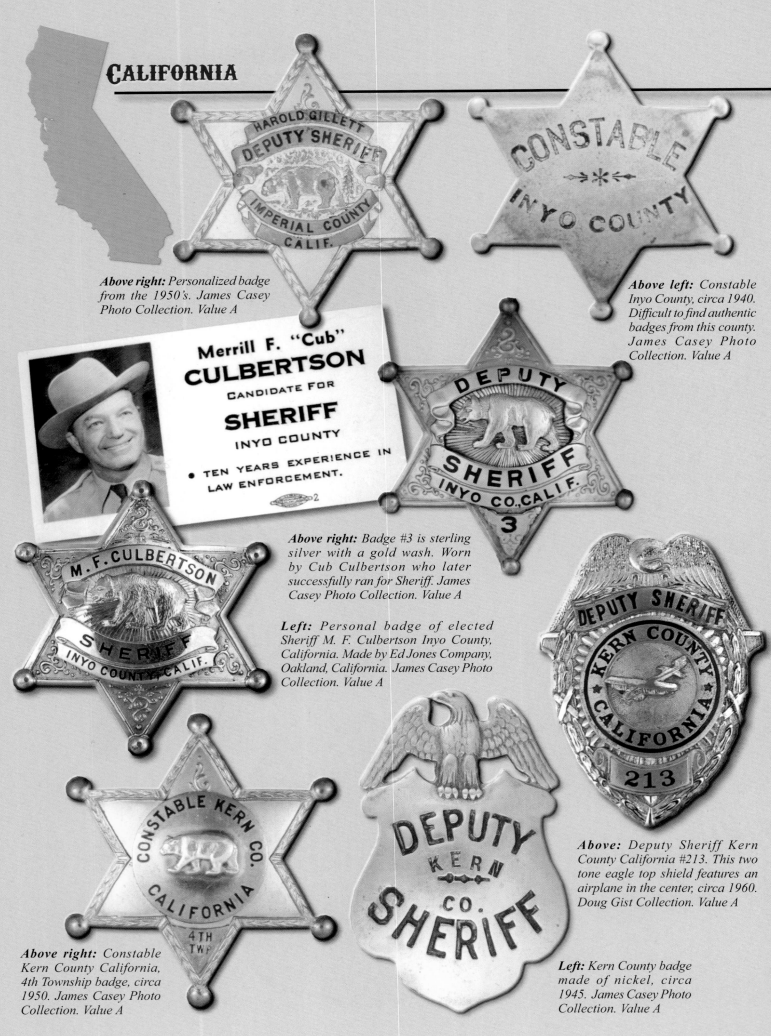

Above right: Personalized badge from the 1950's. James Casey Photo Collection. Value A

Above left: Constable Inyo County, circa 1940. Difficult to find authentic badges from this county. James Casey Photo Collection. Value A

Merrill F. "Cub" **CULBERTSON** CANDIDATE FOR **SHERIFF** INYO COUNTY • TEN YEARS EXPERIENCE IN LAW ENFORCEMENT.

Above right: Badge #3 is sterling silver with a gold wash. Worn by Cub Culbertson who later successfully ran for Sheriff. James Casey Photo Collection. Value A

Left: Personal badge of elected Sheriff M. F. Culbertson Inyo County, California. Made by Ed Jones Company, Oakland, California. James Casey Photo Collection. Value A

Above: Deputy Sheriff Kern County California #213. This two tone eagle top shield features an airplane in the center, circa 1960. Doug Gist Collection. Value A

Above right: Constable Kern County California, 4th Township badge, circa 1950. James Casey Photo Collection. Value A

Left: Kern County badge made of nickel, circa 1945. James Casey Photo Collection. Value A

DEPUTY *LASSEN COUNTY* **SHERIFF**

Above: Hard to find authentic Lassen County badge, made of nickel, circa 1935. James Casey Photo Collection. Value A

R. L. MARR JR. UNDERSHERIFF LAKE COUNTY

Above: R. L. Marr Jr. wore this gold front badge and later became Chief of Police in Anderson, California. James Casey Photo Collection. Value A

DEPUTY SHERIFF LAKE COUNTY

Above: A young Walter Mills working as a Imperial County, California deputy sheriff. James Casey Collection.

Left: Nickel silver Lake County badge, circa 1920. James Casey Photo Collection. Value A

21

Above: Captain, Los Angeles, Detective. 14k gold multi layered gold adorned with two diamonds. Presented To Paul W. Schenck From His Many Friends Of The Los Angeles Police Department Detective Bureau May 15 1925, Z 14K. Private Collection. James Casey photo. Value D

Right: Los Angeles City policeman wears 1st issue eight point star #20. Photographer Golsh. James Casey Collection.

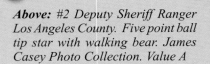

Above: #2 Deputy Sheriff Ranger Los Angeles County. Five point ball tip star with walking bear. James Casey Photo Collection. Value A

Above right: Dual titled Constable Los Angeles County, California and Deputy Sheriff. Nickel silver circa 1900. James Casey Photograph. Value B

Above: Eagle Rock, California, Desk Sergeant Police #1, located in Los Angeles County, circa 1920. James Casey Photograph. Value A

Right: Police Patrolman 7 Huntington Park - A gold color shield with hard fired blue enamel lettering. A very unusual shaped badge from yesteryear. Photograph by Godfrey Gigiorgi. Al Mize Collection. Value A

Above: Deputy City Marshal #41, City of Vernon, located in Los Angeles County, circa 1915. James Casey Photograph. Value A

22

Right: Chas. E. Rice Constable Los Angeles, 14k gold, jeweler made. Presentation reads: "From His Friends – 1908" Private Collection. James Casey Photograph. Value E

Left: Los Angeles #5 Police. A rare second issue Los Angeles police badge with hard fired black enamel. Doug Gist Collection. Value D

Above: Los Angeles City policeman wearing a 1st issue eight point star. James Casey Collection.

Above: Deputy Sheriff Los Angeles County, California #1, sterling silver, hard fired black enamel. Jeweler made, circa 1920. James Casey Photograph. Value C

Above right front and back: Deputy Constable #1 Belvedere Township, Los Angeles County, California, hard fired blue enamel. Baseball center design. James Casey Photograph. Value B

CALIFORNIA

Right: Los Angeles City policeman wearing a 1st issue eight point star #45. James Casey Collection.

Above front and back: LA City #9 Police. One of the most sought after first issue badges from the Los Angeles police department. Doug Gist Collection. Value E

Above: Los Angeles City policeman wearing a 1st issue eight point star #70 strikes a handsome pose. James Casey Collection.

Right: Policewoman Santa Monica Police Record Bureau. Al Mize Collection. Value A

Left: Constable L.A.T. (Los Angeles Township) Los Angeles County, J.C.C. (John C. Cline) sterling silver, jeweler made, hand cut letters, T-Pin, C catch. James Casey photo. Value D

Above: July 6, 1915, Chief of Police, City of Los Angeles, founded 1781. A gold badge presented to Clarence E. Snively in 1915. John Boessenecker Collection. Value D

Left: Venice, California #1 Police, nickel silver with applied copper number, circa 1920. James Casey Photograph. Value B

Above: Deputy Sheriff, 146, Los Angeles County, California- A silver color eagle top shield with hard fired black enamel lettering and light engraving in the shield. This regular deputy badge was used from 1900-1919 when they went to the bear top shield that only lasted for one term. A real old and rare badge. Photograph by Godfrey Gigiorgi. Al Mize Collection Hallmark: "Chipron Stamp Co., 224 W. First St., Los Angeles." Value B

Above: Captain Walter J. Mills of the Venice California police department. James Casey Collection.

25

Left: Deputy Sheriff L. A. County California, german silver, hard fired black enamel, baseball center design, 2". James Casey Photograph. Value A

Above: C. M. Baldwin L.A. County Deputy Sheriff. A gold Los Angeles deputy sheriff badge, worn by C.M. Baldwin, circa 1890s. John Boessenecker Collection.

Right: Secretary To Chief, Los Angeles Police. A gold badge, presented to Clarence E. Snively in 1911. John Boessenecker Collection. Value D

Above: Deputy Marshal E San Gabriel. James Casey Photo Collection. Value A

Above: Cabinet photo of a Pasadena, California police officer wearing a 1st issue badge #3. James Casey Collection.

Above: Los Angeles Captain Police, series two circa 1890 done in sterling silver with reverse hard fired blue enamel. Restored. James Casey Photograph. Value D

26

POMONA PARK 1 POLICE

Left: Pomona Park Police #1, nickel silver, circa 1900. James Casey Photograph. Value A

POLICE 5 OCEAN PARK

Above: Police #5 Ocean Park, California located in Los Angeles County, nickel silver, circa 1900. James Casey Photograph. Value B

CONSTABLE MALIBU TOWNSHIP

Left: Constable Malibu Township. This badge is nickel silver. James Casey Photo Collection. Value A

DEPUTY MARSHAL CITY OF SIGNAL HILL, CAL. 1

Above: Deputy Marshal #1 City of Signal Hill, California. James Casey Photo Collection. Value A

Above: This Los Angeles officer proudly wears his Grand Army of the Republic civil war badge below his 1st issue police badge. James Casey Collection.

Above left: San Rafael Township Constable, located in Marin County California. James Casey Photo Collection. Value A

Above: Constable San Rafael Township, engraved edge, circa 1940. James Casey Photograph. Value A

Above left: City of Madera, California police officer wearing a sterling silver hand engraved badge. James Casey Collection.

Above left: Deputy Sheriff Marin County. James Casey Photo Collection. Value A

Right: Nice old nickel Deputy Sheriff badge from Mariposa County, California, circa 1900. James Casey Photograph. Value B

Left: Deputy Marshal #7 San Anselmo, located in Marin County California, this badge is very collectible and hard to find, circa 1930. James Casey Photo Collection. Value A

28

Left: *Deputy Constable, Anderson District, Mendocino County - A silver color shield with soft black enamel lettering, used in 1930-50 era. Hallmark: "Patrick & Co., SF." Photograph by Godfrey Gigiorgi. Al Mize Collection. Value A*

Right: *Deputy Sheriff Mendocino County with fancy design and hard fired blue enamel surrounding the California walking bear. James Casey Photo Collection. Value A*

Above: *Deputy Sheriff Mendocino done in sterling silver with hard fired blue enamel and hand engraved. This badge was made by Irvine & Jachens, circa 1930. James Casey Photo Collection. Value A*

Below right: *Ukiah 1 Police, large 4" pie plate design, nickel, made by Moise Klinkner Company, San Francisco, circa 1930. James Casey Photograph. Value B*

Above: *The personal badge of Reno Bartolomie, the elected sheriff of Mendocino County. Hard fired blue enamel enhances this gold colored badge. Reno was a twenty year elected sheriff, who held office from 1954-1975. James Casey Photo Collection. Value A*

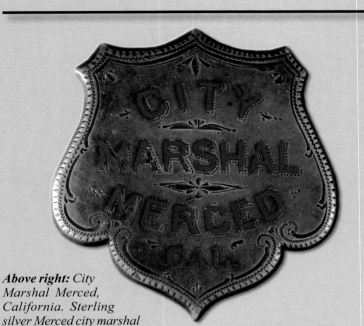

Above right: *City Marshal Merced, California. Sterling silver Merced city marshal badge, hard fired blue enamel, with T-Pin, circa 1870s. John Boessenecker Collection. Value C*

Left: *A rare Jailer badge from Merced County. James Casey Photo Collection. Value A*

Right: *Deputy Sheriff Merced County done in nickel silver and enhanced with stamped in five point stars, circa 1890. James Casey Photo Collection. Value A*

Above right: *Merced 2 Police, circa 1900, interesting stamped designs in the points. James Casey Photograph. Value A*

Left: *Merced County Constable, California, Township 2. German silver, hand chased engraving, hard fired blue enamel. James Casey Photograph. Value B*

Right: *Deputy Sheriff Merced County, made of nickel, circa 1930. Doug Gist Collection. Value A*

Above: Under Sheriff Modoc County with hard fired blue enamel, circa 1970. James Casey Photo Collection. Value A

Above and left front and back: 14k gold Sheriff badge of Modoc County, California. T-Pin, 3", hard fired reverse blue enamel. James Casey Photograph. Value D

Above: Deputy Sheriff Mono County, California. Six point star with soft black enamel, circa 1940. James Casey Photo Collection. Value A

Above: Deputy Sheriff Mono County, California with carnival lettering and block lettering. Hallmarked J. C. Irvine S. F., circa 1896. James Casey Photo Collection. Value B

31

Above left: Deputy Sheriff Monterey County, California in nickel silver with soft black enamel. James Casey Photo Collection. Value A

Above: Constable Mott Township located in Siskiyou County near the railroad town of Dunsmuir. James Casey Photo Collection. Value A

Left: Deputy Sheriff Napa County with fancy stamping in the points. James Casey photo collection. Value A

Above left: Undersheriff Napa County. James Casey Photo Collection. Value A

Imperial county, California, deputy sheriffs. On the left is Walter Mills. The deputy on the right is not identified. James Casey Collection.

Above: Jacob Teeter Deputy Sheriff Nevada County, California, sterling silver, circa 1860, jeweler made, T-Pin. Jacob Teeter was a famous lawman in Truckee, California and was shot and killed in a shootout in Hurd's Saloon by rival lawman James Reed. James Casey Photograph. Value E

Look me carefully over
And if I'm found all right,
Surely you will help me
Win the Sheriff fight.

36

Is your official register number:
I'll guard your welfare
While you slumber.

Efficiency in office shall be your reward.
Sincerely Yours,

R. B. BIDDLE.

Above: Constable Meadow Lake Township, Nevada County, California, silver, hard fired blue enamel with blue stone, hand engraved, made by J. C. Irvine, circa 1896 and last worn by August Schlumpf. James Casey Photograph. Value E

Above: Election campaign card from R. B. Biddle, numbered 36 and includes a poem. James Casey Collection.

Left: Deputy Sheriff badge worn by August Schlumpf in Truckee, California, circa 1890, 2" german silver, gold wash, engraved edge. James Casey Photograph. Value A

Left: Deputy Sheriff Nevada County, California shield cut out star in nickel silver. James Casey Photo Collection. Value A

Above: Classic circle star designed Constable badge used in Meadow Lake Township, Truckee, California, circa 1890. Made of nickel silver. James Casey Photograph. Value B

Above: Deputy Sheriff Nevada County, circa 1920 six point ball tip star. Doug Gist Collection. Value A

Above: Deputy Sheriff Nevada County California circle cut out star in nickel silver. James Casey Photo Collection. Value A

Left: Grass Valley #7 Police - A silver color seven point star with hard fired black enamel lettering. An old badge from this old mining town, used in 1920-1935 era. Photograph by Godfrey Gigiorgi. Al Mize Collection B Hallmark: "Ed Jones & Co. Oakland, Cal. STERLING." Value B

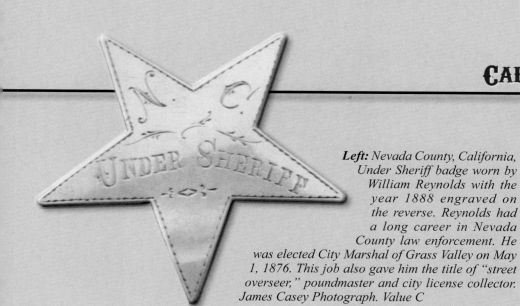

Left: Nevada County, California, Under Sheriff badge worn by William Reynolds with the year 1888 engraved on the reverse. Reynolds had a long career in Nevada County law enforcement. He was elected City Marshal of Grass Valley on May 1, 1876. This job also gave him the title of "street overseer," poundmaster and city license collector. James Casey Photograph. Value C

Wayne Brown Sheriff Nevada County served 32 years and retired in 1982. James Casey photo collection. Value A

Above: City Marshal badge, circle cut out star design in sterling silver. Possibly the badge of Steve Venard of Nevada County, California. James Casey Photo Collection. Value C.

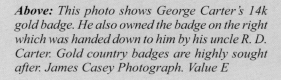

Above: This photo shows George Carter's 14k gold badge. He also owned the badge on the right which was handed down to him by his uncle R. D. Carter. Gold country badges are highly sought after. James Casey Photograph. Value E

Above: This beautiful 14k gold badge was worn by two Nevada County Sheriffs beginning with R.D. Carter in 1882. In 1927 his nephew George Carter was elected Sheriff and had the dates of election added to the badge. James Casey Photograph. Value E

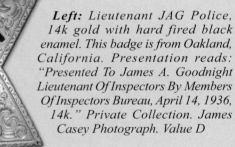

Above front and back: Chief of Police, BAW, Oakland California, owned by Bodie A. Wallman. Inscription reads: "Presented To Chief Bodie A. Wallman By Members Of Oakland Police Dept. 1934 B.J. Co. 14k 18k Platinum." Private Collection. James Casey Photograph. Value D

Left: Lieutenant JAG Police, 14k gold with hard fired black enamel. This badge is from Oakland, California. Presentation reads: "Presented To James A. Goodnight Lieutenant Of Inspectors By Members Of Inspectors Bureau, April 14, 1936, 14k." Private Collection. James Casey Photograph. Value D

Above: 14k Gold Chief Of Police. R. P. T., Oakland, California, adorned with diamonds. Presentation reads: "Presented To Chief Of Police, Robert P. Tracy, By Members Of Oakland Police Dept 1943, B.J. Co. 14k." Private Collection. James Casey Photograph. Value D

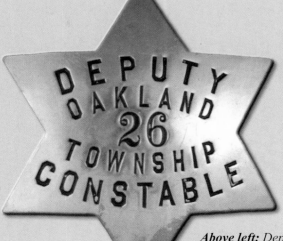

Right: Inspector 65 Police. Sterling silver, hand engraved, hard fired black enamel, 3¼" tall. Made by Pioneer Oakland, California. James Casey collection. Value C

Above left: Deputy Constable #26 Oakland Township badge in nickel silver. James Casey Photo Collection. Value A

Left: This beautifully engraved sterling, Detective Sergeant #7 badge is probably from a city near Oakland, California. This badge is typical of the badges worn in the East Bay. The engraving includes the official flower of California, the Poppy, in the design. Made by Ed Jones, Co. Oakland, California. James Casey Photograph. Value B

Above: Lieutenant R.P.T. (Robert P. Tracy) Inspectors, Oakland, California, 14k gold. Made by Block Jewelery Oakland, California. Private Collection. James Casey Photograph. Value D

Above: Oakland, California Police Sergeant, #244. A nice example of the beautiful engraving the Ed Jones Company was doing in the 1920's and 1930's. Hard fired black enamel. Made by Ed Jones Company, Oakland, California. James Casey Photograph. Value B

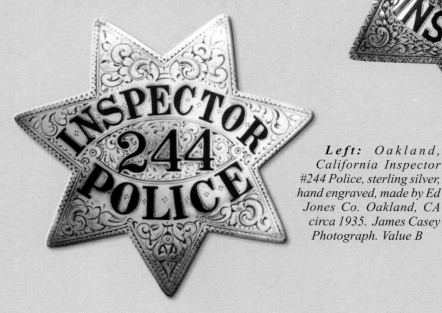

Left: Oakland, California Inspector #244 Police, sterling silver, hand engraved, made by Ed Jones Co. Oakland, CA circa 1935. James Casey Photograph. Value B

Above: Captain RPT (Robert P. Tracy) Inspectors. This Badge is from the Oakland California Police. It has the officers initials monogrammed in the center of the back of the badge. It has hard fired black enamel type and is hand embellished. Presentation reads: "Presented To Rob't. P. Tracy, Aug 7 1940, By Commanding Officers And Members Of Inspectors Bureau , Oakland Police Dept, 14k." Private Collection. James Casey Photograph. Value D

Right: Fay E. Bates Undersheriff Placer County badge with hard fired blue enamel, circa 1958. James Casey Photo Collection. Value A

Above: Wm. Fonseca Constable Placer County badge with hard fired blue enamel, circa 1960. James Casey Photo Collection. Value A

Left front and back: Deputy Sheriff Placer County, 1½" brass, circa 1935. James Casey Photograph. Value A

Above: Deputy Sheriff, Placer County - A silver color circle cut out 5 point star. Used in this historic gold country county of the wild mining camps and expanding settlements. Photograph by Godfrey Digiorgi. Hallmark: Patrick and Moise, K, San Francisco, Cal. Al Mize Collection. Value A

Left: A. T. Stevenson Chief of Police Portola, California badge in gold front and made by the Ed Jones Company, Oakland, California. James Casey Photo Collection. Value A

Above: W. C. Abernethy Jr. Under-Sheriff Plumas County, California, badge in gold front and made by the Ed Jones Company Oakland, California. The center of the badge is adorned with a sterling silver walking bear. Abernethy was elected sheriff in 1954. James Casey Photo Collection. Value A.

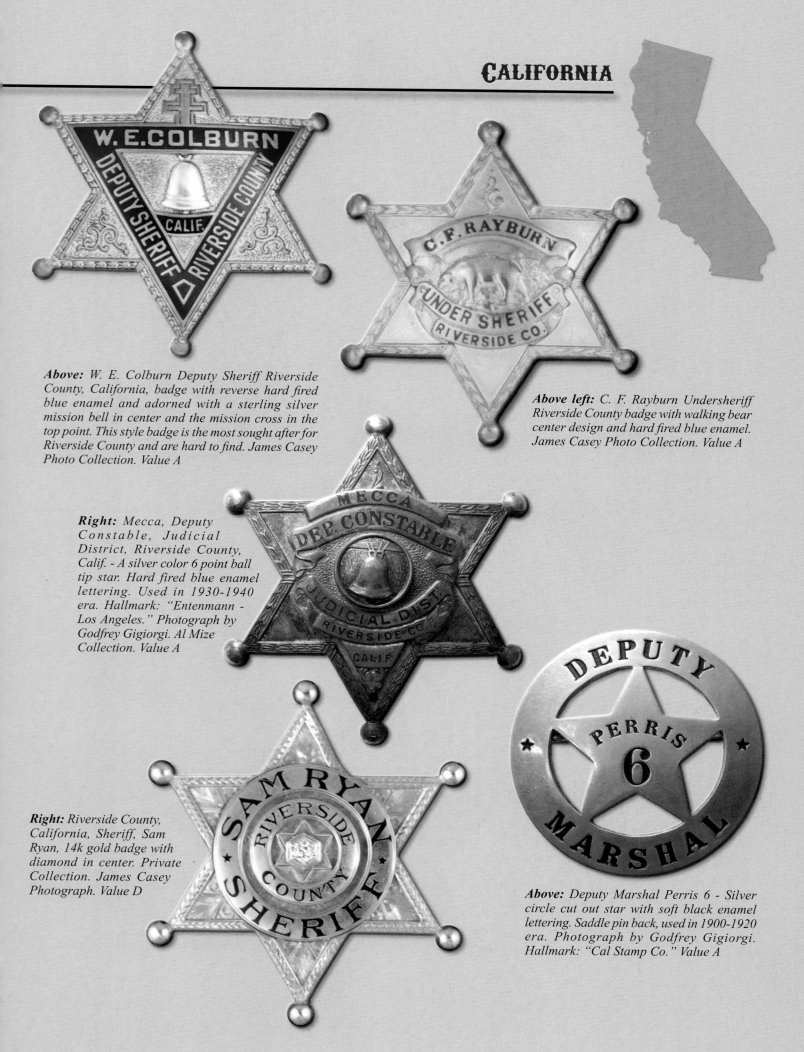

Above: *W. E. Colburn Deputy Sheriff Riverside County, California, badge with reverse hard fired blue enamel and adorned with a sterling silver mission bell in center and the mission cross in the top point. This style badge is the most sought after for Riverside County and are hard to find. James Casey Photo Collection. Value A*

Above left: *C. F. Rayburn Undersheriff Riverside County badge with walking bear center design and hard fired blue enamel. James Casey Photo Collection. Value A*

Right: *Mecca, Deputy Constable, Judicial District, Riverside County, Calif. - A silver color 6 point ball tip star. Hard fired blue enamel lettering. Used in 1930-1940 era. Hallmark: "Entenmann - Los Angeles." Photograph by Godfrey Gigiorgi. Al Mize Collection. Value A*

Right: *Riverside County, California, Sheriff, Sam Ryan, 14k gold badge with diamond in center. Private Collection. James Casey Photograph. Value D*

Above: *Deputy Marshal Perris 6 - Silver circle cut out star with soft black enamel lettering. Saddle pin back, used in 1900-1920 era. Photograph by Godfrey Gigiorgi. Hallmark: "Cal Stamp Co." Value A*

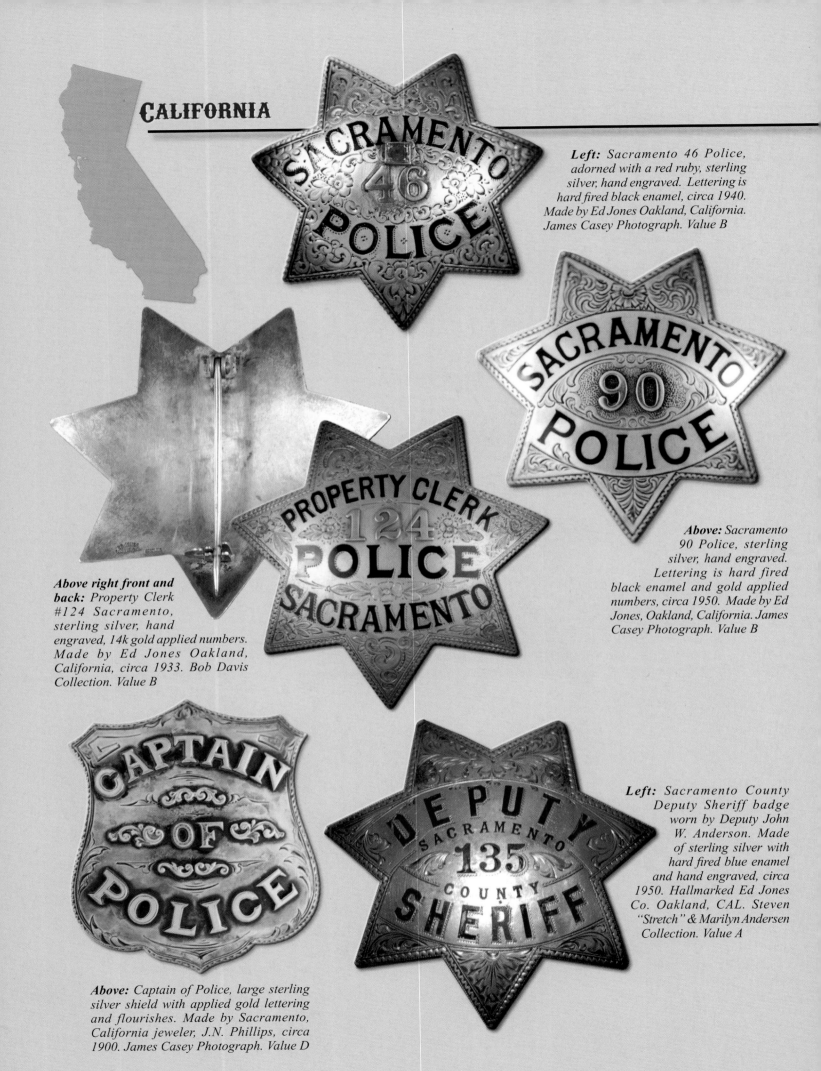

CALIFORNIA

Left: Sacramento 46 Police, adorned with a red ruby, sterling silver, hand engraved. Lettering is hard fired black enamel, circa 1940. Made by Ed Jones Oakland, California. James Casey Photograph. Value B

Above: Sacramento 90 Police, sterling silver, hand engraved. Lettering is hard fired black enamel and gold applied numbers, circa 1950. Made by Ed Jones, Oakland, California. James Casey Photograph. Value B

Above right front and back: Property Clerk #124 Sacramento, sterling silver, hand engraved, 14k gold applied numbers. Made by Ed Jones Oakland, California, circa 1933. Bob Davis Collection. Value B

Left: Sacramento County Deputy Sheriff badge worn by Deputy John W. Anderson. Made of sterling silver with hard fired blue enamel and hand engraved, circa 1950. Hallmarked Ed Jones Co. Oakland, CAL. Steven "Stretch" & Marilyn Andersen Collection. Value A

Above: Captain of Police, large sterling silver shield with applied gold lettering and flourishes. Made by Sacramento, California jeweler, J.N. Phillips, circa 1900. James Casey Photograph. Value D

40

Left: *Sacramento Police #419, sterling silver, hand engraved, 14k gold applied numbers. Made by Ed Jones Oakland, California, circa 1940. Bob Davis Collection. Value B*

Above: *Sacramento, California, police officer wearing a 1st issue badge #10. Photo by Baldwin. James Casey Collection.*

Above: *Chief of Police, Sacramento, California. A silver color seven point star with hard fired black enamel lettering and embellished with awesome hand engraving and hand chasing behind each of the letters, circa 1935. A prestigous badge that would enhance any collection. Hallmark: "Ed Jones Co. Oakland, CA. STERLING." James Casey Photo Collection. Value C*

Above left: *Captain of Police, Sacramento, California, sterling silver, hard fired black enamel, hand engraved and dated 1933. Made by the Ed Jones Company of Oakland, California. James Casey Photograph. Value B*

Left: *Detective Sergeant 5 Police Sacramento, sterling silver and hand engraved. Lettering is hard fired black enamel. Hallmarked Ed Jones 1922. James Casey Collection. Value B*

Above: *Commissioner of Public Health and Safety, Sacramento, California, sterling silver, hand engraved, circa 1915. James Casey Photograph. Value B*

41

Left: Sacramento County Sheriff, 18k gold presentation badge to David Ahern, 1910-1914. Badge was designed by his wife and jeweler made. Hand engraved with black hard fired enamel lettering and a center star with translucent red enamel and a white enameled smaller center star, 2½" James Casey Photograph. Value D

Above: Corporal 10 Police Sacramento, sterling silver, hand engraved, circa 1922. Lettering is hard fired black enamel. Made by Ed Jones Oakland, California. James Casey Photograph. Value B

Right: Detective Sergeant 10 Police Sacramento, sterling silver, hand engraved. Lettering is hard fired black enamel, circa 1933. Made by Ed Jones, Oakland, California. James Casey Photograph. Value C

Above: Early Sacramento, California Sergeant #4 Police badge, circa 1887, made by local jeweler J.N. Phillips. This "pie plate" style badge is made of sterling silver with an applied 14k gold #4 in the center and has hard fired blue enamel lettering that has been shadowed. Generous hand engraving enhances the overall appearance of this old timer. The badge was issued to Sergeant "Pop" Becker. James Casey Collection. Value D

Above: Sheriff Sacramento County, California, 14k gold adorned with a large diamond. Hard fired blue enamel. Presentation reads: "Presented To Ellis Jones From The Boys, 14k." Private collection. James Casey Photograph. Value D

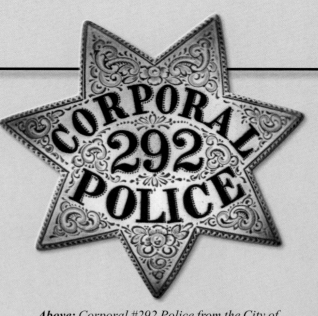

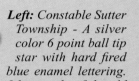

Above: Corporal #292 Police from the City of Oakland, California, circa 1935. This badge is beautifully hand engraved with shadowed lettering in hard fired black enamel. James Casey Photo Collection. Value B

Left: Constable Sutter Township - A silver color 6 point ball tip star with hard fired blue enamel lettering. This is a beautiful example of the old lawman badge that has professional and one of a kind engraving and hand chasing that makes this a magnificent badge. One of my favorites. Hallmark: "Ed Jones & Co., Oakland, Cal. STERLING." Photograph by Godfrey Gigiorgi. Al Mize Collection Value C

Left: Secretary Police Sacramento, sterling silver, hand engraved. Made by Ed Jones Oakland, California, circa 1935. Bob Davis Collection. Value B

Above: Superintendent, Juvenile Department, Police Sacramento, sterling silver, hand engraved, circa 1933. Lettering is hard fired black enamel. Made by Ed Jones Oakland, California. James Casey Photograph. Value C

Right: Patrol Sergeant, 17, Police Sacramento, sterling silver, hand engraved, circa 1933. Lettering is hard fired black enamel. Made by Ed Jones Oakland, California. James Casey Photograph. Value C

Above: Sergeant #281 Police from the City of Oakland, California, circa 1935. This badge is beautifully hand engraved with shadowed lettering in hard fired black enamel. James Casey Photo. Al Mize Collection. Value B

Above left: San Benito County Deputy Sheriff, nickel silver, circa 1940. James Casey Photo Collection. Value A

Above: Deputy Marshal #1 Ontario, California, San Bernardino County, nickel silver with copper applied number, circa 1910. James Casey Photograph. Value B

Above: Policeman San Bernardino Police #16. Al Mize Collection. Value A

Above: Deputy Sheriff San Bernardino County O.R.C. 14k gold. Presentation Reads: "Presented To G.F. Hewins By The 3rd Ward Boosters, May 1 1909, 14k." Private Collection. James Casey Photograph. Value D

Above left and right: Deputy Sheriff San Bernardino County – Two nice examples of the California walking bear design enhance these nickel badges. Doug Gist Collection. Value A

Left: Captain San Clementa Policewoman. Al Mize Collection. Value A

Right front and back: San Diego County, California Deputy Sheriff #29 Sterling silver, stamped design in points. Made by Ed Jones Company Oakland, California, circa 1940. James Casey Photograph. Value B

Above: Deputy Marshal 11 East San Diego, California - A silver color shield cut out 5 point star with soft black enamel lettering. Saddle pin back. Rare and magnificent in its simplicity. Hallmark: "Cal. Stamp Co." Photograph by Godfrey Gigiorgi. Al Mize Collection. Value B

Left: Ernest Dort Sheriff, San Diego County, California. This beautiful 14k gold badge is nicely engraved in the center, custom die design stamping in the points and has hard fired blue enamel. 2½". James Casey Photograph. Value D

Above: Deputy Sheriff 9 San Diego County, California - A silver color seven point star with hard fired blue enamel lettering a light engraving. A real beauty in its own simplicity. Used in 1925-1935 era. This is the first issue of their sterling badge. Hallmarked: "Ed Jones & Co., Oakland, Cal. STERLING." Photograph by Godfrey Gigiorgi. Al Mize Collection. Value B

Right: Deputy Marshal San Diego County - A silver color circle with five point cut out star. Soft black enamel lettering and a old saddle pin back. Used in early 1900's to 1920. Photograph by Godfrey Gigiorgi. Al Mize Collection Hallmarked: "Los Angeles Rubber Stamp." Value B

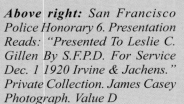

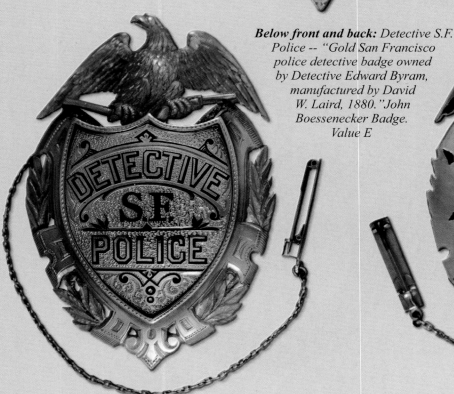

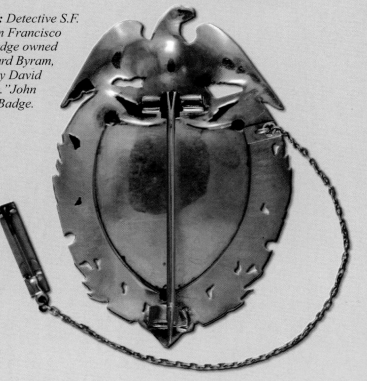

Above: San Francisco Special Police sign made of brass and blue enamel. James Casey Collection.

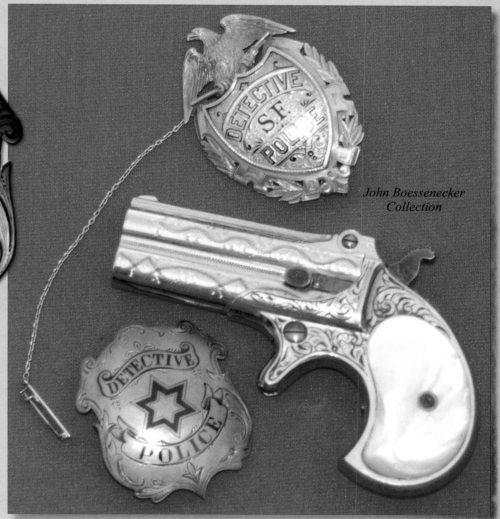

Above: Detective Police. Sterling silver San Francisco police detective badge owned by Detective Edward Byram, manufactured by David W. Laird. John Boessenecker Collection. Value D

John Boessenecker Collection

CALIFORNIA

Right: *Deputy Sheriff San Francisco 192 - A silver color 7 point silver star with a gold color horse's head in the center. Hard fired blue enamel lettering. Used exclusively during the 1939 World's Fair in conjunction with the building of the Golden Gate Bridge. A beauty to behold. Photograph by Godfrey Digiorgi. Hallmark: "Ed Jones & Co., Oakland, Cal. Gold Front." Al Mize Collection. Value A*

Above: *Sergeant #94 Police badge made of sterling silver with hard fired blue enamel. Possibly from the San Francisco bay area, circa 1890. James Casey Photo Collection. Value A*

Left: *San Francisco County, California Deputy Sheriff #132, 14k gold. Private Collection. James Casey Photograph. Value C*

Above: *Captain 508 S.F. Police, 14k gold, hand engraved. Presentation Reads: "Capt. Walter F. Ames From Members Of His Platoon Co. E., March 15-49." Private Collection. James Casey Photograph. Value D*

Above left: *San Francisco, California, police officer wearing a 1st issue badge #514. Photo by Goden's. James Casey Collection.*

48

Above: G.W. Blum was the San Francisco Police Department photographer. It was his job to present to each new Chief of Police the framed photos of the former chiefs and marshals of the city. Officer Blum would create a large framed "City Marshal's and Chief's of Police" group photo to hang in the Chief's office. The picture above was Blum's masterpiece in 1911 and is signed by him. It measures four feet wide and just over three feet tall. Hand painted design surrounds each individual photo. James Casey Collection. Value D

Above: Detective Sergeant #244. This San Francisco badge is done in sterling silver and 14k gold applied numbers with hard fired blue enamel. Hand engraved. Dated 8-25-07, Irvine W. & Jachens Sterling. James Casey Collection. Value D

Above: Rare and early San Francisco Detective badge, sterling silver, hard fired black enamel. T-pin and C catch, circa 1875. One of two known to exist. James Casey Photograph. Value D

49

Above: *San Francisco 793 Police USA (United States Army). This 14k gold badge was presented to a San Francisco Police officer upon his return from serving in World War One. Presentation reads: "Presented To Daniel J. O'Neill By Members Of Co. E., S.F.P.D., JULY 17, 1918, Irvine & Jachens Private Collection. James Casey Photograph. Value D*

Above and right, front and back: *Retired San Francisco # A 87 Police 14k gold presentation badge, made by Irvine & Jachens. James Casey Photo Collection. Value B*

Right: *San Francisco Pie Plate style badge #30 in sterling silver. T-pin and C catch, circa 1875. James Casey Photograph. Value B*

Right: *Captain Officer Morse's Patrol. Gold badge, made by Shreve Company and presented in 1889 to Captain Jules J. Callundan of Harry Morse's Detective and Patrol Agency in San Francisco." John Boessenecker Collection. Value D*

Above: *Sergeant #3138 S. F. Police Reserve badge in sterling silver with hard fired blue enamel. James Casey Photo Collection. Value A*

50

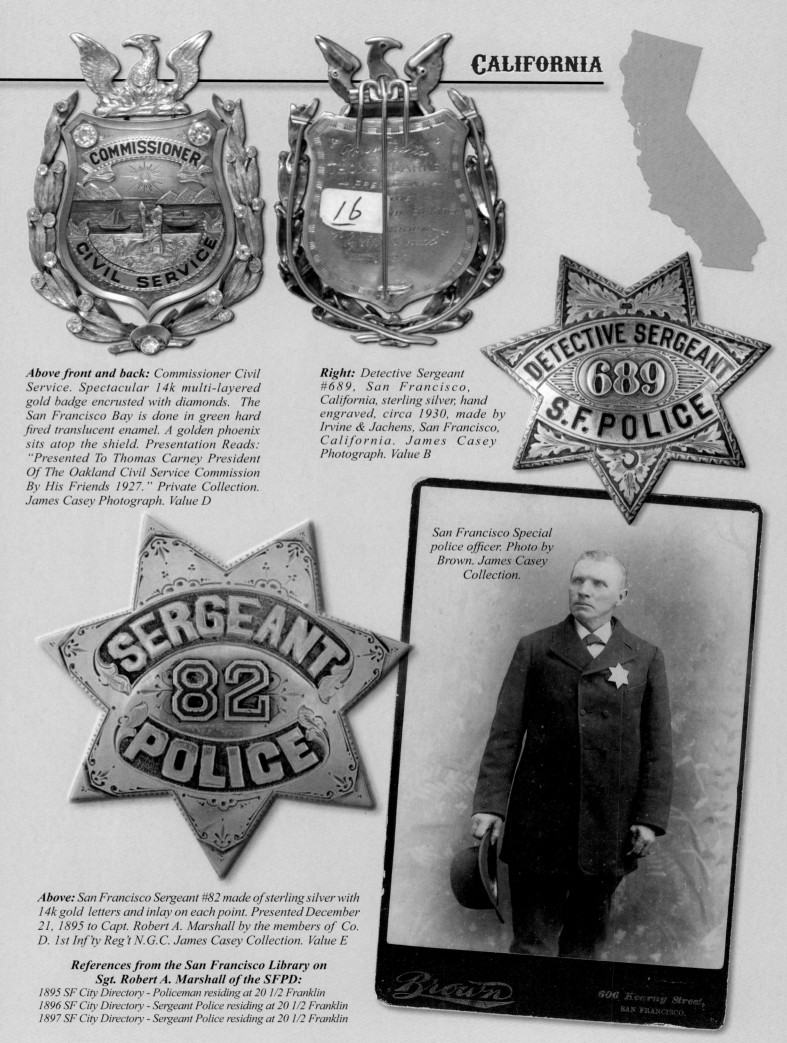

Above front and back: *Commissioner Civil Service. Spectacular 14k multi-layered gold badge encrusted with diamonds. The San Francisco Bay is done in green hard fired translucent enamel. A golden phoenix sits atop the shield. Presentation Reads: "Presented To Thomas Carney President Of The Oakland Civil Service Commission By His Friends 1927." Private Collection. James Casey Photograph. Value D*

Right: *Detective Sergeant #689, San Francisco, California, sterling silver, hand engraved, circa 1930, made by Irvine & Jachens, San Francisco, California. James Casey Photograph. Value B*

San Francisco Special police officer. Photo by Brown. James Casey Collection.

Above: *San Francisco Sergeant #82 made of sterling silver with 14k gold letters and inlay on each point. Presented December 21, 1895 to Capt. Robert A. Marshall by the members of Co. D. 1st Inf'ty Reg't N.G.C. James Casey Collection. Value E*

References from the San Francisco Library on Sgt. Robert A. Marshall of the SFPD:
1895 SF City Directory - Policeman residing at 20 1/2 Franklin
1896 SF City Directory - Sergeant Police residing at 20 1/2 Franklin
1897 SF City Directory - Sergeant Police residing at 20 1/2 Franklin

Above front and back: *San Francisco, California Sergeant #677, sterling silver, hand engraved, circa 1930, made by Irvine & Jachens S.F. CAL. James Casey Photograph. Value B*

Left: *Very rare and beautifully engraved Stockton, California Police Detective #7, sterling silver, made by the Ed Jones Co. Oakland, California, circa 1927. James Casey Collection. Value C*

Above: *Deputy Sheriff, San Joaquin County, California #8. Sterling silver and hand engraved with hard fired blue enamel. Made by Glick Jewelry Stockton, California, circa 1900. James Casey Photograph. Value C*

Below left: *Admission Day Celebration Stockton California N.S.G.W. (Native Sons Golden West) Sept. 9, 1883. 14k gold. Private Collection. James Casey Photograph. Value C*

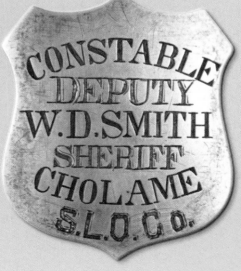

Above: *Benjamin Franklin Rogers Chief of Police Stockton California 18k gold, hand cut lettering. Presentation reads: "Presented Dec. 24, 1884." Private Collection. James Casey Photograph. Value D*

Right: *Constable W. D. Smith Cholame badge in sterling silver. The title "Deputy Sheriff S.L.O. (San Luis Obispo) Co." were added at a later date. Cholame is where actor James Dean died in a car crash September 30, 1955. James Casey Photo Collection. Value B*

Above: *This forerunner to the California Highway Patrol was used in Sacramento County. Made by Irvine & Jachens Co. circa 1928. Nickel silver. James Casey Photograph. Value A*

Right: *Deputy Constable San Mateo County badge in nickel silver. Hallmarked Will & Finck San Francisco. James Casey Photo Collection. Value B*

Sheriff's Office, San Mateo County, Calif.

THIS IS TO CERTIFY THAT ___ W W Coovert ___ is a duly appointed DEPUTY SHERIFF of San Mateo County, and full faith and credit are due all his official acts as such.

WITNESS my hand and seal this __24__ day of ___ June ___, 19__48__

Expires ___ Jan. 1951 ___   James J. McGrath
                                              Sheriff

Right: *Police 4 Redwood City, San Mateo County, California, hard fired blue enamel, circa 1930. James Casey Photograph. Value A*

Above: *Mounted Patrol Deputy Sheriff, San Mateo County, 139. A beautiul and historic 7 point star with hard fired blue enamel and a gold color eagle riveted in the center of the badge. This unit was disbanded years ago and the badge brought pride to its owner. Photograph by Godfrey Digiorgi Hallmarked: "Olsen-Nolte, San Francisco, CA STERLING & 1/10 10k gold filled." Al Mize Collection. Value B*

Left: *San Mateo County, California, Deputy Sheriff, 14k gold. Private Collection. James Casey Photograph. Value C*

53

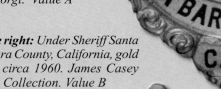

Left: Deputy Sheriff #5 San Mateo County, nickel silver, circa 1900, James Casey Photo Collection. Value A

Above left: Deputy Coroner San Mateo County, nickel silver, circa 1950. James Casey Photo Collection. Value A

Left: Captain Peninsula Mounted Patrol Deputy Sheriff, San Mateo County. Beautiful gold filled presentation badge with hard fired blue enamel. 2¾". Presentation reads: "Howard Guttman. Hallmarked Irvine & Jachens Gold Filled." Al Mize Collection. Photograph by Godfrey Digiorgi. Value A

Above right: Under Sheriff Santa Barbara County, California, gold filled, circa 1960. James Casey Photo Collection. Value B

Above: Deputy Sheriff San Mateo County #93. Gold front with hard fired blue enamel, 3". Hallmarked: "Gold Front." Al Mize Collection. Photograph by Godfrey Digiorgi. Value A

Above: Deputy Constable LaGrange Township, nickel silver, circa 1936. James Casey Photo Collection. Value A

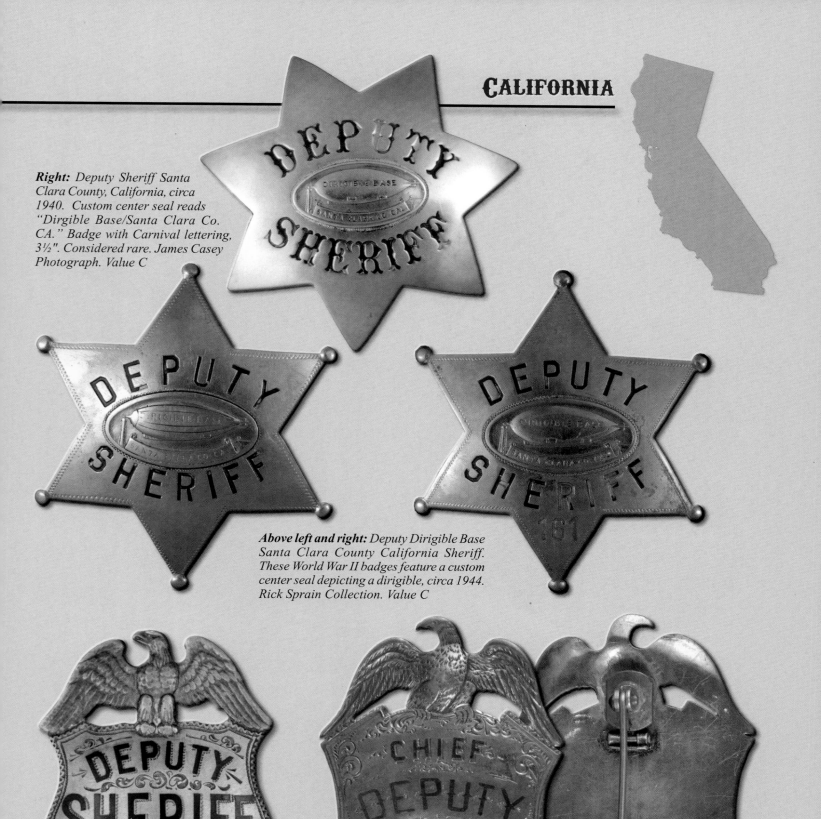

Right: Deputy Sheriff Santa Clara County, California, circa 1940. Custom center seal reads "Dirgible Base/Santa Clara Co. CA." Badge with Carnival lettering, 3½". Considered rare. James Casey Photograph. Value C

Above left and right: Deputy Dirigible Base Santa Clara County California Sheriff. These World War II badges feature a custom center seal depicting a dirigible, circa 1944. Rick Sprain Collection. Value C

Above: Deputy Sheriff Santa Clara County California. Badge in sterling silver, hard fired blue enamel and hand engraved, shadowed lettering, 3". James Casey Photograph. Value B

Above front and back: Chief Deputy Sheriff Santa Clara County. Sterling silver, hand engraved, hard fired blue enamel, circa 1900. Verso, T-Pin, C catch. Rick Sprain Collection. Value C

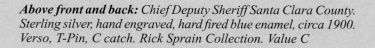

55

CALIFORNIA

Above: Sheriff's Sergeant Santa Clara County #93 badge in sterling silver and hard fired blue enamel. *James Casey Photo Collection. Value A*

Above: Constable Redwood Township Santa Clara County. *Rick Sprain Collection. Value A*

Above: Inspector Sheriff's Department, Santa Clara County #122. *James Casey Photo Collection. Value A*

Left: Deputy Sheriff Santa Clara County, California, nickel silver, 2", circa 1930. All of the designs on the this badge are part of the die. *James Casey Photograph. Value A*

Above front and back: Deputy Sheriff Santa Clara County. Sterling silver, hand engraved, Verso-1919. *Rick Sprain Collection. Value C*

56

Left: Constable San Jose Township badge in nickel silver. James Casey Photo Collection. Value A

Above: Deputy Constable San Jose Township Santa Clara County badge in sterling silver and hard fired blue enamel. This nicely engraved badge is circa 1930. James Casey Photo Collection. Value B

Right: Deputy Constable San Jose Township, circa 1905, nickel silver. James Casey Photograph. Value A

Above: Deputy Sheriff Santa Clara County, California, badge, circa 1940. James Casey Photo Collection. Value A

Above: San Jose, California, Chief of Police image by Hill & Watkins San Jose, California. James Casey Collection.

57

Above front and back: Under Sheriff Santa Clara County. Sterling silver, hand engraved, hard fired blue enamel, circa 1900. Verso, T-Pin, C catch. Rick Sprain Collection. Value C

Above: Deputy Sheriff Santa Clara County badge in sterling silver with a sterling California state seal and hard fired blue enamel lettering. James Casey Photo Collection. Value A

Above: City Marshal Gilroy, California in Santa Clara County, 14k gold. Presentation reads: "Present A.B. Ward By His Friends June 6-1904." Private Collection. James Casey Photograph. Value D

Above front and back: Deputy Sheriff Santa Clara County. Sterling silver, hand engraved, hard fired blue enamel, circa 1895. Verso Hallmarked: "J. C. Irvine." Rick Sprain Collection. Value C

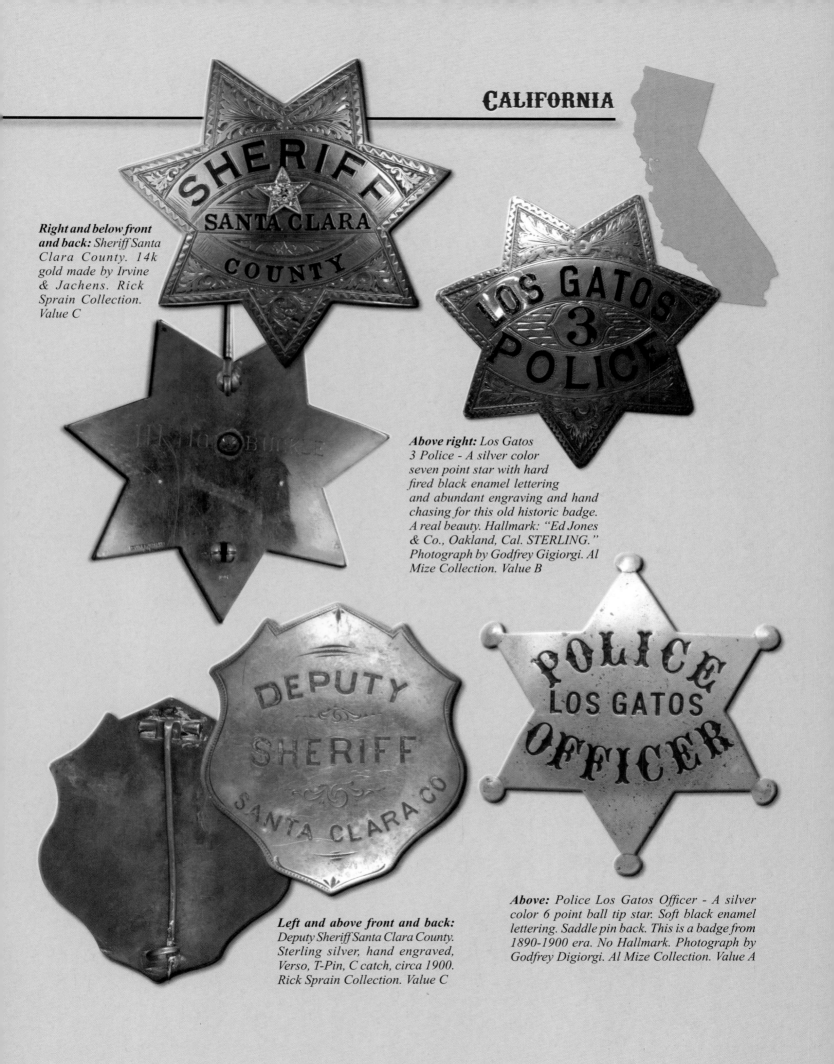

Right and below front and back: *Sheriff Santa Clara County. 14k gold made by Irvine & Jachens. Rick Sprain Collection. Value C*

Above right: *Los Gatos 3 Police - A silver color seven point star with hard fired black enamel lettering and abundant engraving and hand chasing for this old historic badge. A real beauty. Hallmark: "Ed Jones & Co., Oakland, Cal. STERLING." Photograph by Godfrey Gigiorgi. Al Mize Collection. Value B*

Left and above front and back: *Deputy Sheriff Santa Clara County. Sterling silver, hand engraved, Verso, T-Pin, C catch, circa 1900. Rick Sprain Collection. Value C*

Above: *Police Los Gatos Officer - A silver color 6 point ball tip star. Soft black enamel lettering. Saddle pin back. This is a badge from 1890-1900 era. No Hallmark. Photograph by Godfrey Digiorgi. Al Mize Collection. Value A*

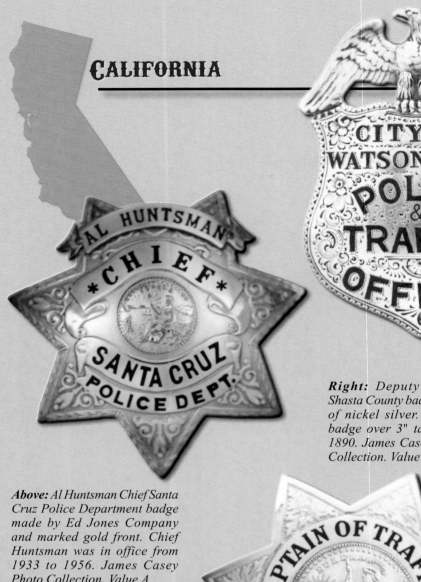

Left: City of Watsonville, California Police & Traffic Officer badge in sterling silver with hard fired blue enamel. This dual titled badge is beautifully hand engraved. Made by the Ed Jones Company of Oakland, California, circa 1930. James Casey Photograph.

Right: Deputy Sheriff Shasta County badge made of nickel silver. A large badge over 3" tall, circa 1890. James Casey Photo Collection. Value A

Above: Al Huntsman Chief Santa Cruz Police Department badge made by Ed Jones Company and marked gold front. Chief Huntsman was in office from 1933 to 1956. James Casey Photo Collection. Value A

Above: Captain of Traffic Redding California badge made by Ed Jones Company, Oakland, California and marked gold front, circa 1960. Photo courtesy of retired Captain Bobby G. Coulter. Value A

Above left: Sierra County Sheriff badge marked Sterling on the back. James Casey Photo Collection. Value A

Above: City Marshal. Redding California, 14k gold and hand engraved with hard fired black enamel, circa 1887. The gold used to make this badge was probably mined locally as Redding in Shasta County, was a robust gold producing area. Private Collection. James Casey Photograph. Value D

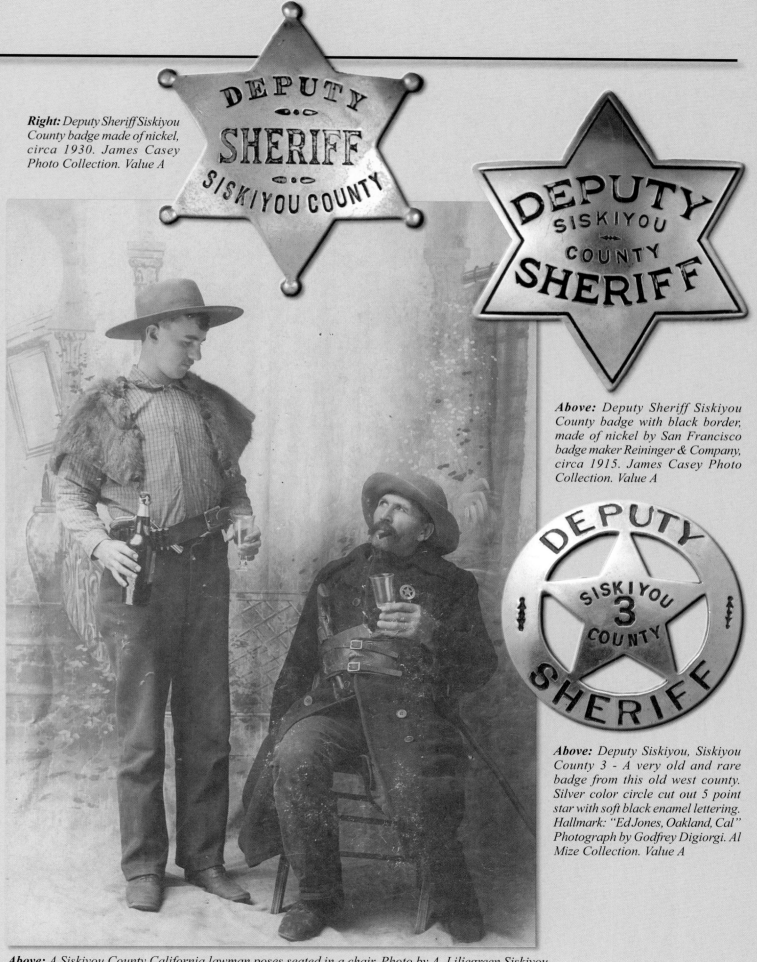

Right: Deputy Sheriff Siskiyou County badge made of nickel, circa 1930. James Casey Photo Collection. Value A

Above: Deputy Sheriff Siskiyou County badge with black border, made of nickel by San Francisco badge maker Reininger & Company, circa 1915. James Casey Photo Collection. Value A

Above: Deputy Siskiyou, Siskiyou County 3 - A very old and rare badge from this old west county. Silver color circle cut out 5 point star with soft black enamel lettering. Hallmark: "Ed Jones, Oakland, Cal" Photograph by Godfrey Digiorgi. Al Mize Collection. Value A

Above: A Siskiyou County California lawman poses seated in a chair. Photo by A. Liljegreen Siskiyou County, California. James Casey Collection.

61

Above: Campaign election card from Siskiyou County, California for the office of Sheriff. Andrew Calkins was the incumbent in this election. James Casey Collection.

Above: Stunning 14k gold Sheriff of Siskiyou County, California. Multi layered gold with hard fired blue enamel. Personal badge of A.S. Calkins. The gold used to make this badge was from the Calkins family mine located in Siskiyou County, circa 1924. Private Collection. James Casey Photograph. Value E

Above: This sterling silver, hand engraved badge was worn by Sheriff Charles B. Howard who held the office from 1902-1918. The abbreviation DEPT at the top of the badge stands for Department not Deputy. This badge was in the collection of former Siskiyou Sheriff Al Cottar who served as sheriff from 1950-1976 and previously was Chief of Police in Dunsmuir, Special Agent for the S.P.R.R. and an F.B.I. agent. In the 1960's Sheriff Cottar had a copy of the badge made for the descendents of Sheriff Howard. James Casey Photograph. James Casey Collection. Value D

Above: Siskiyou County, California, Sheriff B.F. Walker, 14k. Private Collection. James Casey Photograph. Value D

Left: *Deputy Solano County Sheriff - A nice old circle cut out 5 point star with soft black enamel lettering. A badge of the old west. Saddle pin back. Hallmark: "Ed Jones & Co., Oakland." Photograph by Godfrey Digiorgi. Al Mize Collection. Value A*

Right: *Constable Cordelia - A silver color shield with soft black enamel lettering. Used in this old and historic town located in Solano County. Known as a stopping off place for the Railroad. Hallmark: "J. C. Irvine - 339 Kearney St., SF." James Casey Photograph, Al Mize Collection. Value B*

Above: *Solano County Sheriff's Air Squadron # 1F8, 1 ½", circa 1950. James Casey Photograph. Value A*

Left: *Deputy Sheriff Sonoma County badge made of nickel silver. James Casey Photo Collection. Value A*

Above: *Deputy Sheriff Sonoma County #5 made of sterling silver and hallmarked Irvine & Jachens 1027 Market Street, S. F., circa 1925. James Casey Photo Collection. Value A*

Above: *Sheriff Sonoma County, California. Presentation reads: "Presented To E. Douglas Bills By His Deputies And Friends Feb. 1927." Private Collection. James Casey Photograph. Value D*

Left: *Sheriff Sonoma County, California. Gold Sonoma County sheriff badge, presented to Sheriff Frank P. Grace in 1899. John Boessenecker Badge. Value C*

63

Above front and back: Deputy Sheriff Stanislaus County, California. Nickel silver, with baseball design in center, circa 1940. Made by L.A. Rubber Stamp Co. L. A. CAL. James Casey Photograph. Value A

Right: L. F. Mallory Under Sheriff, Stanislaus County, California, circa 1880, sterling silver, jeweler made, enamel in both blue and black, hand engraved. James Casey Photograph. Value D

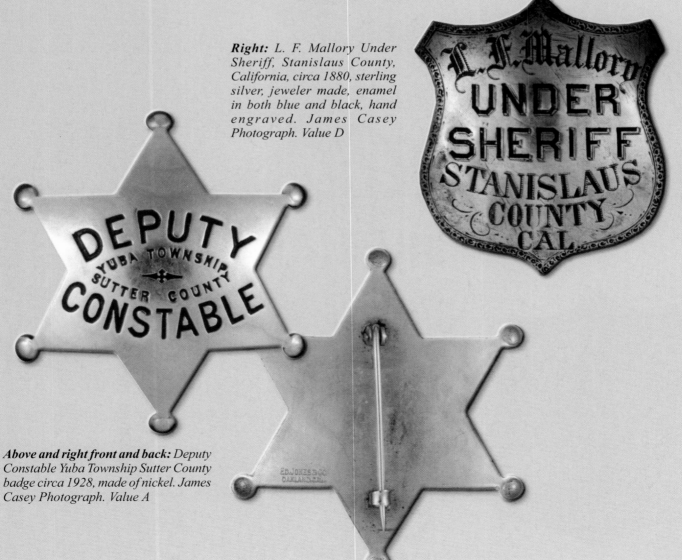

Above and right front and back: Deputy Constable Yuba Township Sutter County badge circa 1928, made of nickel. James Casey Photograph. Value A

Left: *Deputy Sheriff Tehama County, nickel silver six point ball tip star, circa 1940. James Casey Photo Collection. Value A*

Right: *Deputy Sheriff Tehama County, nickel silver shield, circa 1910. James Casey Photo Collection. Value A*

COUNTY OF TEHAMA
EMPLOYEE IDENTIFICATION

Name Lyle Williams
Dept. Sheriff' Office
Title Sheriff
Sex Male   Age 44
Hair Brown Wgt. 260
Eyes Green Hgt. 6'

I.D. NO.
45

Signature of Employee

Above, right and below: *The Sheriff and Undersheriff badges and employee identification of Lyle Williams of Tehama County. James Casey Photo Collection. Value of both badges A*

Above: *Red Bluff Police. Large six point ball tip badge from Red Bluff, California, circa 1920. Doug Gist Collection. Value A*

Right: *Nickle over brass circle cut out star from Trinity County, Circa 1915. James Casey Photo Collection. Value B*

65

Left: Deputy Sheriff Tuolumne County #6, circa 1945. James Casey Photo Collection. Value A

Above left: Constable Woodville Precinct Tulare County, nickel silver, circa 1935. James Casey Photo Collection. Value A

Right: Policeman Farmersville Police #1, circa 1960. James Casey Photo Collection. Value A

Left front and back: World War II vintage Ventura County Deputy Sheriff #45, sterling silver. James Casey Photograph. Value A

Above: Constable PIRU Ventura County, nickel silver, made by LA Rubber Stamp Company, circa 1910. James Casey Photo Collection. Value A

Left and below front and back:
Ventura County California, Deputy Sheriff, made of nickel silver, hallmarked "STP. CO." James Casey Photograph. Value A

Left and above front and back:
Jeweler made Ventura County Deputy Sheriff, circa 1890. James Casey Photograph. Value B

Two badges to the left and above, front and back:
Unique and rare two sided badge. Originally worn by William Kelly as a Deputy Sheriff in Dakota County, Nebraska. He then moved to Ventura County, California. The badge was then taken to a jeweler and made into a Ventura County, California Deputy Sheriff badge. Sterling silver, circa 1880. James Casey Photograph. Value D

CALIFORNIA

68

Right: Railroad and Steamboat Police #696 California Southern Pacific Company, circa 1925, sterling silver with hard fired blue enamel. Made by Irvine & Jachens San Francisco. James Casey Photograph. Value B

Above: Photographer J. B. Shane traveled town to town by rail car. Here he captures the images of two railroad police officers. James Casey Collection.

Above: This Southern Pacific railroad officers cap reads, "State R.R. Police S. P. Co." and his badge is a 1st issue railroad and steamboat badge. James Casey Collection.

Right: State of California Railroad Police Southern Pacific #76 Steamboat Police. 1st issue, circa 1890. James Casey Photo Collection. Value A

Above left: State Humane Officer of California 2, made of sterling silver with hard fired blue enamel, circa 1917 by Irvine & Jachens. Value A

69

COLORADO

Above: Colorado Rangers #2 badge. The Colorado Rangers operated from 1861 to January 29, 1923. Courtesy Ron Donoho. Value B

SHAW,   115 W. Fourth Street,
               PUEBLO, COLO.

Above: *Pueblo, Colorado police officer. James Casey collection.*

Left: *Denver police officer wearing 2nd issue badge #38. Wright photographer. James Casey Collection.*

Above: *Pueblo, Colorado Police No. 1, done in silver. This classic design was used in Pueblo in the 1880's. James Casey Photograph. Value C*

70

Left: Denver police officer wearing second issue badge # 4. Wright photographer. James Casey Collection.

Right: Wm W. Arnett City & County of Denver Sheriff Chief Deputy 14k gold suspension badge. James Casey Photo Collection. Value D

CONNECTICUT

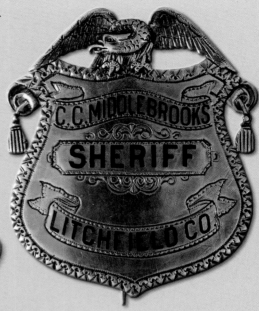

Left: Bridgeport, Connecticut Police, circa 1875, 2nd Sergeant Rank, gold plated. Ernie Leves Collection. Value B

Above: Police, Meriden, Connecticut, circa 1885. Ernie Leves Collection. Value A

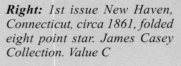

Above: New Haven, Connecticut, 2nd Issue, circa 1860's. Ernie Leves Collection. Value A

Above: New Britain Police. Unique shield, german silver, circa 1900. James Casey Collection. Value A

Above: Eugene F. Crosby City Sheriff City of Waterbury Connecticut.- A unique gold color eagle top shield with hard fired blue enamel lettering and custom seal center. A beauty of the east coast. No Hallmark. Photograph by Godfrey Digiorgi. Al Mize Collection. Value A

Right: 1st issue New Haven, Connecticut, circa 1861, folded eight point star. James Casey Collection. Value C

72

HAWAII

Left: Detective County of Hawaii, circa 1950. Private Collection. Value B

Above: Gold Sheriff of Hawaii, T-Pin, circa 1894. Private Collection. Value D

Above: Police 17 Kauai - A silver color circle with cut out five point star. A real beautiful and magnificent badge of this rare state. Light engraving highlights. Used in 1900-1920 era on Kauai, Hawaii. Awesome. Hallmarked: "STERLING." Photograph by Godfrey Gigiorgi. Al Mize Collection. Value C

Above: Investigator Public Prosecutor C&C (City and County) Honolulu, TH, (Territory of Hawaii), circa 1940. Private Collection. Value B

Above: Police Clerk 3 S. Hilo County of Hawaii, circa 1940. Private Collection. Value B

Left: Gold Sheriff of Oahu, T-Pin, circa 1852. Private Collection. Value E

Above: Traffic Captain County of Hawaii, T.H. (Territory of Hawaii) Police, circa 1940. Private Collection. Value B

73

IDAHO

Right: Deputy Game Warden Idaho, nickle silver, circa 1950. James Casey Photo Collection. Value A

DEPUTY — GAME WARDEN — IDAHO

PAYETTE POLICE

Above: Payette Police badge made of nickel silver. James Casey Photo Collection. Value A

Right: Butte City 17 Police, a large nickel badge, circa 1890. James Casey Photograph. Value B

BUTTE CITY 17 POLICE

Above: Imperial sized cabinet card photo of a Boise, Idaho police chief. James Casey Collection.

Below front and back: Chicago Police 1820. 14k gold. Presentation reads: "From Members Of 8th District Retired June 22nd 1936 To John White. Private Collection. James Casey Photograph. Value D

Above: Police #167 Chicago. Chicago Police 1st issue, known as the "flat badge" with the Childs Company first hallmark, circa 1870. James Casey Collection. Value B

Below right: City of Chicago Police #197, second issue, known as the Chicago coat shield. Gary Provenzano Collection. Al Tukey Photograph. Value A

ILLINOIS

Above: Danville, Illinois officer wearing a circle cut out star badge. Phillips & Bergstresser photographer. James Casey Collection.

Above: Sangamon Sheriff 14k Gold. Hallmark reads: "Presented To Meredith J. Rhule Dec 2 1946 From His Friends Made By Wexler." Private Collection. James Casey Photograph. Value D

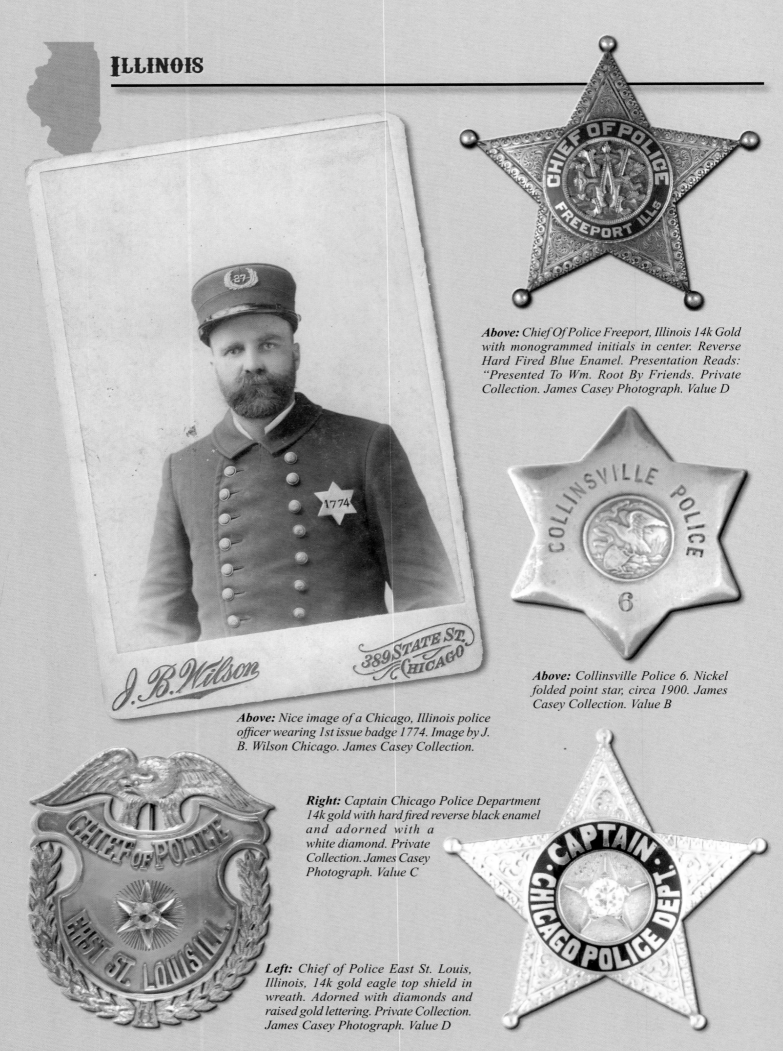

Above: Chief Of Police Freeport, Illinois 14k Gold with monogrammed initials in center. Reverse Hard Fired Blue Enamel. Presentation Reads: "Presented To Wm. Root By Friends. Private Collection. James Casey Photograph. Value D

Above: Nice image of a Chicago, Illinois police officer wearing 1st issue badge 1774. Image by J. B. Wilson Chicago. James Casey Collection.

Above: Collinsville Police 6. Nickel folded point star, circa 1900. James Casey Collection. Value B

Right: Captain Chicago Police Department 14k gold with hard fired reverse black enamel and adorned with a white diamond. Private Collection. James Casey Photograph. Value C

Left: Chief of Police East St. Louis, Illinois, 14k gold eagle top shield in wreath. Adorned with diamonds and raised gold lettering. Private Collection. James Casey Photograph. Value D

INDIANA

Below left: *Indianapolis Police #80. A third issue 6-point star badge. Gary Provenzano Collection. Al Tukey Photograph. Value A*

Above: *14k Gold Suspension Badge. Sheriff of Marion County Isaac King. Presentation reads: "Presented By His Deputies." Private Collection. James Casey Photograph. Value D*

Above right: *This Lafayette, Indiana, officer wears an impressive and unique badge. Photographer Lawson & Bros. La Fayette, Indiana. James Casey Collection.*

Right: *14k Gold Sheriff Lake County Indiana. Beautiful inlaid gold with hard fired blue enamel. Presentation reads: "To Lee B. Clayton From Deputies 1947-1950, 14k." Private Collection. James Casey Photograph. Value D*

Above: *14k Gold Sheriff Lake County, Indiana. Beautiful inlaid gold with hard fired blue enamel adorned with red stone. Presentation Reads: "Presented To Jack West By His Friends 1951. The C.H. Hanson Co. Chicago 14k." Private Collection. James Casey Photograph. Value D*

77

Left: Des Moines Civil Service Police Sergeant. A 6-point star, circa 1909. Gary Provenzano Collection. Al Tukey Photograph. Value A

Below: Des Moines Police Detective, circa 1904. Gary Provenzano Collection. Al Tukey Photograph. Value A

Above: This officers hat reads GUARD. John Bellew photographer Anamosa, Iowa. James Casey Collection.

Above: Nice image of the Marshal of Cedar Rapids, Iowa taken by the Cottage Studio. James Casey Collection.

IOWA

Right: Sheriff of Humboldt County Iowa, sterling silver, hand chased, circa 1920. James Casey Photograph. Value C

Above: Sherraden studio in Council Bluffs, Iowa captured this image of the Supt. of the Fire & Police Telegraph. James Casey Collection.

Left: *Constable Crawford County Kansas. Interesting badge design, circa 1920. James Casey Photograph. Value A*

Right: *14k gold Captain Police Department K.C.K (Kansas City Kansas), with hard fired black enamel. Private Collection. James Casey Photograph. Value D*

KANSAS

Right: *Chief Of Police, Winfield Kansas. 14k gold with reverse hard fired blue enamel, adorned with the American Eagle and the Federal Crest. Presentation reads: "To Brother James McLam By Winfield Lodge 732 B.P.O.E. 6-1-1904 FCH 12-10-28." Private Collection. James Casey Photograph. Value D*

Left: *L. W. Hoover Sheriff Cowley County Kansas. 14k gold with hard fired black enamel. Private Collection. James Casey Photograph. Value D*

Above: *A Kansas lawman poses wearing a suspension badge. Photo by Downing, Topeka, Kansas. James Casey Collection.*

Right: *Wichita Police #68. A five-point star, circa 1937-1953. Classic Art Deco, designed by Captain Ray Ashworth. Made by Dorset. Gary Provenzano Collection. Al Tukey Photograph. Value A*

79

LOUISIANA

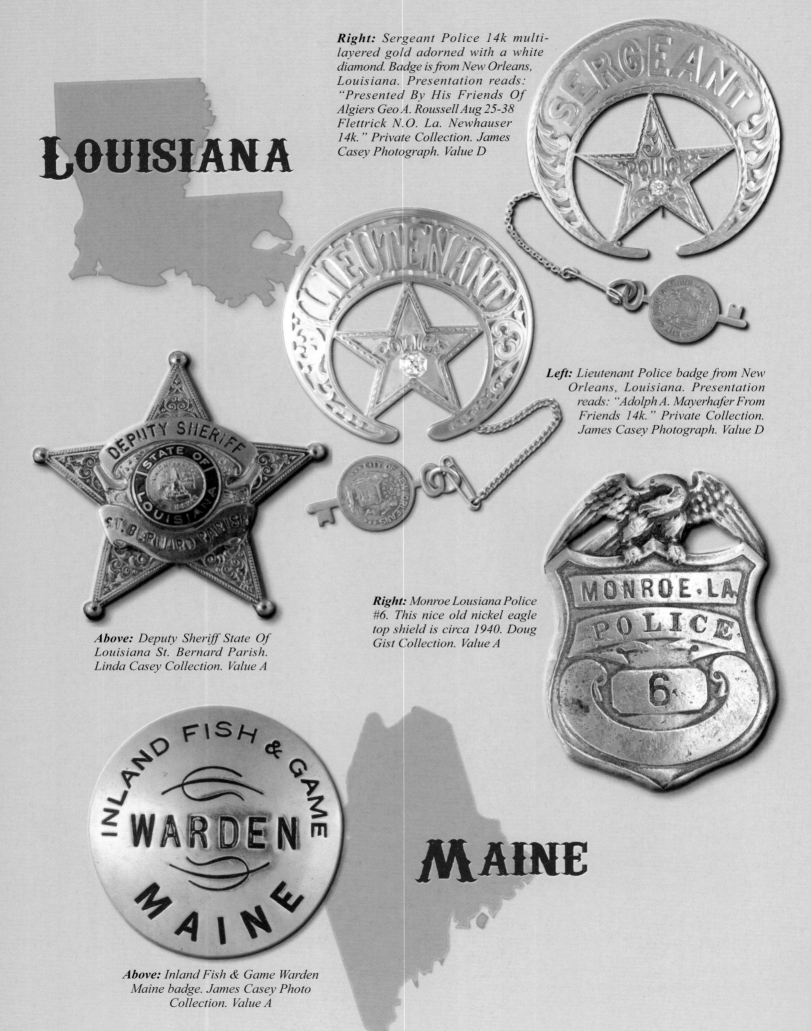

Right: Sergeant Police 14k multi-layered gold adorned with a white diamond. Badge is from New Orleans, Louisiana. Presentation reads: "Presented By His Friends Of Algiers Geo A. Roussell Aug 25-38 Flettrick N.O. La. Newhauser 14k." Private Collection. James Casey Photograph. Value D

Left: Lieutenant Police badge from New Orleans, Louisiana. Presentation reads: "Adolph A. Mayerhafer From Friends 14k." Private Collection. James Casey Photograph. Value D

Above: Deputy Sheriff State Of Louisiana St. Bernard Parish. Linda Casey Collection. Value A

Right: Monroe Lousiana Police #6. This nice old nickel eagle top shield is circa 1940. Doug Gist Collection. Value A

MAINE

Above: Inland Fish & Game Warden Maine badge. James Casey Photo Collection. Value A

Below right: Baltimore, Maryland police officer wearing 1st issue police badge, circa 1851.

Above: Baltimore Police 2nd issue badge, circa June 1860. This is a large oval shield measuring 4" tall and 3" wide. The center of the badge depicts the traditional Roman fasces which consisted of a bundle of birch rods, tied together with a red ribbon into a cylinder, and including an axe amongst the rods. James Casey Collection. Value C

MARYLAND

Above: Very rare 1st issue Baltimore police badge. One of five known to exist. As reported by The Sun Baltimore October 21, 1851 "Page 1, Local Matters: The Stars.–The badge designed to be worn by the city police was yesterday mounted for the first time by Messrs. McKinley & Calloway, who are in special attendance at the hall of the Maryland Institute. It consists of a heavily gilded, brightly burnished six pointed star, in the centre of which is seen a correct representation of the Battle Monument, surrounded by the words "City Police," and underlined with the date of "1797" the date of our city's charter. The star is worn on the left lappel of the coat, and is so conspicuous that he who runs may read." James Casey Collection. Newspaper article courtesy of Gary Provenzano. Value D

Left: Baltimore Police 3rd issue badge (1st style) issued June 22, 1862. These badges were made with the 1st issue center seal and are two piece construction with a brass ring and points, 3" tall. The second style 3rd issue went to one piece white metal construction as the two piece construction was more expensive. It is thought that the majority of the 1st issue badges were cannibalized to remove the center seal for use in the new 2nd issue. This theory has merit since only five first issue Baltimore badges are known to exist. James Casey Collection. Value B

MASSACHUSETTS

Above: So. Danvers Police - 1st issue badge used from 1855 to 1866. The city name then changed to Peabody. Obverse: T-pin, C-catch. James Casey Collection. Value C

Above: Peabody Police - 1st issue badge, circa 1866, of the newly named City of Peabody, (formerly So. Danvers.) James Casey Collection. Value B

Right: J. Henry Davis was a Boston photographer who captured this image of a Boston police officer wearing a "radiator" style badge. James Casey Collection.

288 BOYLSTON ST.

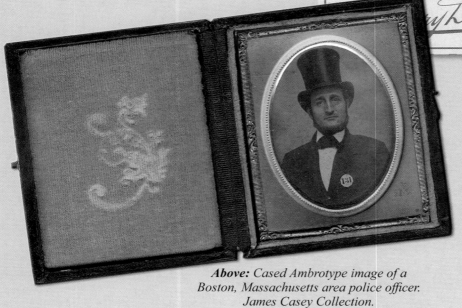

Above: Cased Ambrotype image of a Boston, Massachusetts area police officer. James Casey Collection.

Above: Boston Police - 5th issue badge used from October 1, 1870 until 1890. Obverse: T-pin, C-catch. James Casey Collection. Value C

Left: Malden, Massachusetts Police Chief. J. W. Dyer Photographer. James Casey Collection.

Right: New Bedford 31 Police - A silver color round badge with soft black enamel lettering and the number cut out of the center of the badge. A beautiful and unique badge from 1890-1900. No Hallmark. Photograph by Godfrey Digiorgi. Al Mize Collection. Value A

Left: Somerville, Massachusetts police officer wearing badge #36. James Casey Collection.

Above: Captain Portsmouth Police - Radiator style, circa 1880. James Casey Collection. Value A

Right: Cambridge Police - Radiator style, circa 1880. James Casey Collection. Value A

Above: Boston 1st issue police badge, circa 1853. James Casey Collection. Value D

83

MICHIGAN

Above: Metropolitan Police Detroit - Early and rare example of a metropolitan police badge. Doug Gist Collection. Value A

Right: Cabinet card photo of a Battle Creek, Michigan police officer. James Casey Collection.

84

MINNESOTA

Above: St. Paul, Minneapolis, Minnesota police officer. Photo by Schiattman Brothers. James Casey Collection.

SCHLATTMAN BROS.   271, E. 7th St. ST. PAUL, MINN.

Left: *Minneapolis #1240 Police. A plain and simple shield with soft black enamel. Doug Gist Collection. Value A*

Right: *Minneapolis Police #34. Six-point star with lettering that could be be stamped or engraved. Gary Provenzano Collection. Al Tukey Photograph. Value B*

Above: *St. Paul #14 Police. A classic shield with cut out star design. Doug Gist Collection. Value A*

Above: *St. Paul Police #70. First issue star, circa 1890. Gary Provenzano Collection. Al Tukey Photograph. Value B*

Right: *Cabinet card image of the Chief of Police of Thief River Falls, Minnesota. James Casey collection.*

85

Left: Cabinet photo of a St. Louis, Missouri, metropolitan police officer. James Casey Collection.

Above: Deputy Game & Fish Commissioner Missouri. Obverse inscribed: "R. W. Steinke St. Louis Mo. Jan. 14, 1920." James Casey Collection. Value A

MISSOURI

Left: Deputy Sheriff St. Louis County 89. Hallmarked: "Steiner St. Louis Union Seal." James Casey Collection. Value A

Right: St. Louis Captain of Police, circa 1900, from St. Louis, Missouri. Gary Provenzano Collection. Al Tukey Photograph. Value B

Above: Assistant Chief Police, Poplar Bluff, Missouri. Hallmarked: "Russell Uniform Co. New York." Linda Casey Collection. Value A

86

Right: *City Marshal Stover, Missouri, circa 1915, nickel silver. James Casey Photograph. Value A*

Left: *Chief Of Police Kansas City Missouri 14k Gold. Presentation reads: "Bernard C. Brannon" Private Collection. James Casey Photograph. Value D*

Left: *Moberly Chief Police J.L. 14k gold with hard fired black enamel. Presentation reads: "Friend's To J.C. Lynch April 19th 1880." Private Collection. James Casey Photograph. Value D*

Above: *Sheriff - Beautiful 14k gold, hard Fired black enamel, hand engraved. Presentation reads: "John C. Day Springfield Mo. 1891." Private Collection. James Casey Photograph. Value D*

Left: *Kansas City, Missouri police sergeant. Thomson Photographer. James Casey Collection.*

87

MONTANA

Above: *Dawson County Deputy Sheriff made of brass with nickel plate. James Casey Photo Collection. Value A*

Above: *The Solem Studio in Butte, Montana, captured this image of one of Butte's finest wearing a large six-point star. James Casey Collection.*

Above: *Nice image of a Bozeman, Montana, police chief. James Casey Collection.*

NEBRASKA

Left: *Morrill County Nebraska Deputy Sheriff, nickel silver six-point star. James Casey Photo Collection. Value A*

Above: *Police Humboldt Nebraska classic circle cut out star design in. German silver over brass, circa 1900. James Casey Collection. Value A*

Above: *State of Nebraska G. F. & P (Game Fish & Parks) Commission #4 badge. James Casey Photo Collection. Value A*

Left: *Plattsmouth, Nebraska officer #1. Photographer Leonard. James Casey Collection.*

89

Right: *Deputy Game Warden Pershing County, Nevada - A nice old circle cut out five-point star with soft black enamel lettering, circa 1900-1920. Saddle pin back. Hallmark: "Salt Lake Stamp Co." Photograph by Godfrey Digiorgi. Al Mize Collection. Value A*

Above: *Fallon #3 Police circle cut out five-point star made of nickel silver, circa 1930. James Casey Photo Collection. Value A*

NEVADA

Left: *Washoe County Deputy Game Warden, made of brass with nickel plating, circa 1950. James Casey Photo collection. Value A*

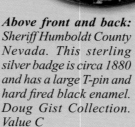

Above front and back: *Sheriff Humboldt County Nevada. This sterling silver badge is circa 1880 and has a large T-pin and hard fired black enamel. Doug Gist Collection. Value C*

Above: *Sheriff Eureka County, Nevada personalized badge of Stanley Fine. James Casey Photo Collection. Value B*

Above right: *Sheriff Nye County, Nevada. Sterling silver with a gold wash center. James Casey Photo Collection. Value B*

Right: Police Conway New Hampshire #8. Eagle top shield design, circa 1930. Doug Gist Collection. Value A

NEW HAMPSHIRE

C. L. HUNT,
Franklin Falls, N. H.
Jeweler & Photographer.

Above: Franklin Falls, New Hampshire officer. C.L. Hunt Jeweler & Photographer. James Casey Collection.

Right: Manchester Police. Commonly referred to as a stop sign design for this Manchester badge. Doug Gist Collection. Value A

Above: Chief Alton Police badge, from Alton, New Hampshire, circa 1930. James Casey Photograph. Value A

91

Left: Police Commissioner Jersey City 1912. 14k gold adorned with a white diamond. Hard fired reverse blue enamel. Presentation reads: "Presented To John F. Sheehan FEB'Y 15, 1912 By His Friends." Private Collection. James Casey Photograph. Value D

NEW JERSEY

Right: Cranford, New Jersey, Police Detective, circa 1870-1880's. This is the only known example. Ernie Leves Collection. Value B

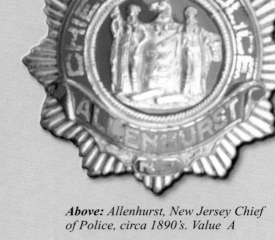

Above: Allenhurst, New Jersey Chief of Police, circa 1890's. Value A

Left: Wallington, New Jersey, Police, Lieutenant, circa 1890's. Value A

Right: City Of Hudson, New Jersey 1st Issue (and only issue) 1855-1869. In 1869 the city of Hudson was incorporated into Jersey City, New Jersey. This is the only known example. Ernie Leves Collection. Value B

92

Left: Newark Police #46, circa 1885-1900, this third issue badge is done in the classic radiator style, made of nickel silver. Gary Provenzano Collection. Al Tukey Photograph. Value A

Left: This officer wears a winter uniform and holds a baton. James Casey Collection.

Above: Hoboken, New Jersey Police, Detective Sergeant, gold plated, circa 1890. Ernie Leves Collection. Value A

Above: Newark Police #12. This is the second issue Newark, New Jersey badge, circa 1865-1885. Gary Provenzano Collection. Al Tukey Photograph. Value B

Left: Westfield, New Jersey Police, 1st Issue, circa 1850's, only example known. Note the officers name engraved on lower front. Ernie Leves Collection. Value A

Above: Morristown, New Jersey Chief of Police, circa 1890's. Ernie Leves Collection. Value A

93

NEW JERSEY

BENJAMIN MURPHY
Chief of Police, Jersey City

EDWARD REILLY
Inspector of Police, Brooklyn

Above: A pair of vintage tobacco trading cards featuring prominent police officers. James Casey Collection.

Above: Sheriff Hudson County, New Jersey. 14k gold with hard fired reverse blue enamel. Adorned with a red stone. Private Collection. James Casey Photograph. Value D

Above: Pompton Lakes, New Jersey Police, Sergeant, circa 1930's. Ernie Leves Collection. Value A

Above: Undersheriff Hudson County, New Jersey. 14k gold with hard fired reverse blue enamel. Adorned with a gemstone. Presentation reads: "Presented To Joseph W. Buckley By Friends April 6 1922 14k Dieges & Clust." Private Collection. James Casey Photograph. Value D

Above: Morristown, New Jersey Mounted Police, circa 1890, brass with bronze top. Ernie Leves Collection. Value A

Left: West Hoboken, New Jersey Detective Lieutenant, circa 1890's-1900. This department disbanded in 1921 when West Hoboken was absorbed by Union City, New Jersey. Ernie Leves Collection. Value A

94

New Mexico

Left: *Pat F. Garrett Sheriff Dona Ana County, New Mexico. A gold watch fob with chain. John Boessenecker Collection. Value E*

Above: *P. Caputo Chief of Police Las Cruces badge. James Casey Photo Collection. Value A*

Left: *Photographer J. C. Burge of Kingston, New Mexico took this photo of a retired and vacationing famous lawman Heck Thomas. James Casey Collection.*

Left: Binghamton, New York Police, circa 1860's. This is the only known example. Ernie Leves Collection. Value B

NEW YORK

Right: Brooklyn Police, Roundsman, 28th Precinct, circa 1890. Ernie Leves Collection. Value C

Above: Brooklyn Police Detective, eagle top, circa 1880's. Ernie Leves Collection. Value C

Above and right front and back: Deputy Sheriff Bronx County. 14k gold with reverse hard fired blue enamel. Presentation reads: "Presented To Arthur G. Murphy By The First Sheriff Of Bronx County Solid Gold Dieges & Clust." Private Collection. James Casey Photograph. Value D

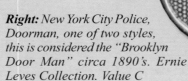

Right: New York City Police, Doorman, one of two styles, this is considered the "Brooklyn Door Man" circa 1890's. Ernie Leves Collection. Value C

96

Form 106-11-28-1902-300

b5117

State of New York,

OFFICE OF THE SECRETARY OF STATE. } ss.:

It is hereby Certified, That the Commission by the Governor of said State, appointing _Daniel Ryan_ a _Steamboat_ POLICEMAN, for the _Baltimore and Ohio Railroad_ Company, and the oath of office of said Policeman were filed in this office this day, under the provisions of Section 58, Chapter 565, Laws of 1890.

Witness, my hand and the Seal of office of the Secretary of State, at the City of Albany, this _10th_ day of _August_ in the year of our Lord one thousand nine hundred and _three._

J. S. Morgan

Deputy, Secretary of State.

Above: Hard to find appointment certificate for a Steamboat policeman. Issued by the State of New York to Daniel Ryan for the Baltimore and Ohio Railroad. James Casey Collection.

Above: Brooklyn Police, Detective, acorn style, circa 1870's. Ernie Leves Collection. Value C

Above: Brooklyn New York Police, Captain, circa 1890. Ernie Leves Collection. Value C

Above: Long Island City Police, (Queens, New York), circa 1890. Ernie Leves Collection. Value C

97

NEW YORK

Right: Second issue Brooklyn Metropolitan Police #18, circa 1857-1870 with original chain keeper. James Casey Collection. Value D

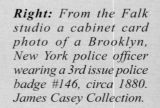

Right: From the Falk studio a cabinet card photo of a Brooklyn, New York police officer wearing a 3rd issue police badge #146, circa 1880. James Casey Collection.

Above: New York City, Metropolitan Police, Captain, 1857-1870, gold plate. Ernie Leves Collection. Value C

Right: New York City Police Inspector, 1880's. Ernie Leves Collection. Value C

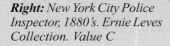

Above: This badge is a third issue Brooklyn, New York police badge, circa 1870-1892 with applied copper numbers 150. James Casey Collection. Value C

Above: Cohoes, New York Police, circa 1860's. Ernie Leves Collection. Value A

Above: 1869 Solid Gold, Commissioner of Police, New Year City, Benjamin F. Manierre. One of a kind! Ernie Leves Collection. Value D

Above: Cold Spring Police, New York, circa 1870, Metropolitan Police Style. Ernie Leves Collection. Value A

Left: New York City Constable, 1857, 18th Patrol District. Only known example of this type of shield. Ernie Leves Collection. Value C

Above right: This very rare 1st issue New York Municipal police badge is number 28, complete with chain keeper, and was issued in 1845. At this time California was part of Mexico, Texas and Florida were just granted statehood and pioneers began following the Oregon trail to settle what was known as Oregon Country controlled by Great Britain and the United States. James Casey Collection. Value D

Right: New York City Detective, maltese cross style, very rare, gold plate, circa 1890's. Only four are known to exist. Ernie Leves Collection. Value C

99

CITY OF
NEW-YORK, } ss.

BY WILLIAM F. HAVEMEYER,

№ 767

MAYOR OF THE CITY OF NEW-YORK.

TO ALL TO WHOM THESE PRESENTS SHALL COME, Greeting:

Know Ye, That *Robert F. Mitchell* having been duly nominated for **Policeman,** under the Act entitled "An Act to amend an Act entitled an Act for the Establishment and Regulation of the Police of the City of New-York," passed May 13th, 1846, and having duly subscribed and taken the Constitutional Oath of Office before me, as required by the said Act, I DO hereby appoint the said *Robert F. Mitchell* to the said Office of **Policeman.**

Given under my hand, at the Mayor's Office, this _____ 16th _____ day of _____ Dec'r _____ one thousand eight hundred and forty *eight*

W. F. Havemeyer MAYOR.

Above and left front and back: City of New York Police Captain. 14k gold with reverse blue enamel and adorned with diamonds. Presentation reads: "Presented To Captain Byron R. Sackett By The Members Of 50th Pct. N.Y.P.D. In Honor Of His Retirement April 16, 1938 Tiffany & Co. 14k." Private Collection. James Casey Photograph. Value D

100

Anderson

785 BROADWAY, N.Y.

Above: The most interesting feature of this cabinet photo of a New York City police captain is the ivory eagle top baton peaking out of the bottom right of the image. Photographer Anderson. James Casey Collection.

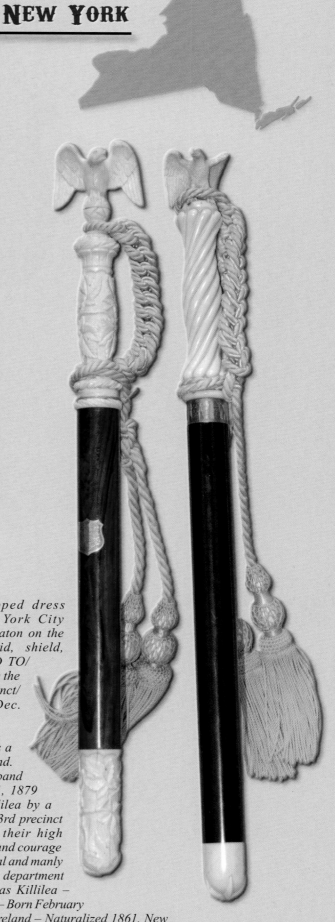

Right: Two ivory topped dress batons from the New York City police department. The baton on the left has a 14k gold inlaid, shield, inscribed, "PRESENTED TO/ CAPTAIN/John Cooney/by the Members of/the 20th. Precinct/ NEW YORK POLICE/Dec. 27th. 1900." Value D

The baton on the right has a 14k gold presentation band. Presentation on the gold band reads as follows: "Jan. 1, 1879 - Presented to Capt. Killilea by a few of his friends in the 33rd precinct as a slight evidence of their high appreciation of his ability and courage as an officer and of his social and manly qualities as a friend." The department record for Captain Thomas Killilea – Assignment: 22nd Precinct – Born February 6, 1838 – Place of Birth Ireland – Naturalized 1861, New York – Appointed October 1, 1866 – Retired February 19, 1901 – Residence 321 W. 59th Street New York. Value E

Above: Wm. H. Craig Sheriff Monroe County New York. 14k gold with raised gold lettering. Private Collection. James Casey Photograph. Value C

101

Above: New York City Municipal Police, acorn style, Ptlm. 1870-72, Badge #2020. Ernie Leves Collection. Value C

Above: New York City Metropolitan Police Inspector, 1857-1870. Ernie Leves Collection. Value C

Right: A very rare 1st issue New York Police Department Assistant Alderman badge made of sterling silver. The inscription on the front of the badge reads: "Timothy R. Hibbard Esq./Asst. Ald. 2nd Ward 1848." James Casey Collection. Value E

Above: Richmond County, New York, Staten Island, Roundsman Metropolitan Police 1857-1870. Ernie Leves Collection. Ernie Leves Collection. Value C

Above right: James W. Moon Sheriff 1910-1912 Herkimer County New York 1916-1916. 14k gold with hard fired black enamel. Private Collection. James Casey Photograph. Value C

Right: New York City, Municipal Police Sergeant, acorn style, 1870-72. Ernie Leves Collection. Value C

Above: New York Police 5th issue Sergeant, circa 1889-1898, commonly referred to as the "Potsy." James Casey Collection. Value D

Left: New York City police Sergeant wearing a "Potsy." Wood Photo Studio. James Casey Collection.

103

Above: Newburgh Police, New York, circa 1870, Metropolitan Style Shield, only three are known to exist. Ernie Leves Collection. Value C

Above: Newburgh Police 37. Washington's Headquarters is proudly displayed in the center of this 1st issue badge, circa 1869. It consists of the Hasbrouck House, the longest-serving headquarters of George Washington during the American Revolutionary War. James Casey Collection. Value C

Above: Municipal Police New York Sergeant. Fourth issue NYPD Sergeants badge, 1875-1889. James Casey Collection. Value C

Left: Police Deppartment City of New York Hostler #18. A custom die badge made by S.A. French, circa 1880. James Casey Collection. Value C

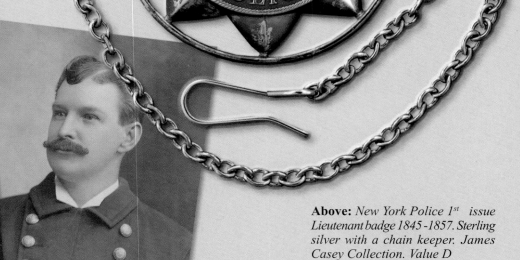

Above: New York police officer William Bailey. James Casey Collection.

Above: New York Police 1st issue Lieutenant badge 1845 -1857. Sterling silver with a chain keeper. James Casey Collection. Value D

Left: New York City police officer wearing a 5th issue badge commonly referred to as the "Potsy." James Casey Collection.

104

Far left: Superintendent of Municipal Police 1874 George W. Walling. This badge is considered by many, the "Holy Grail" of NYPD badges and is well documented in photos and publications. Made by Tiffany & Company in 18k gold. It is one of a kind! Ernie Leves Collection. Value E

Left: Cabinet photo of Superintendent of Police, George W. Walling, New York City. Ernie Leves Collection.

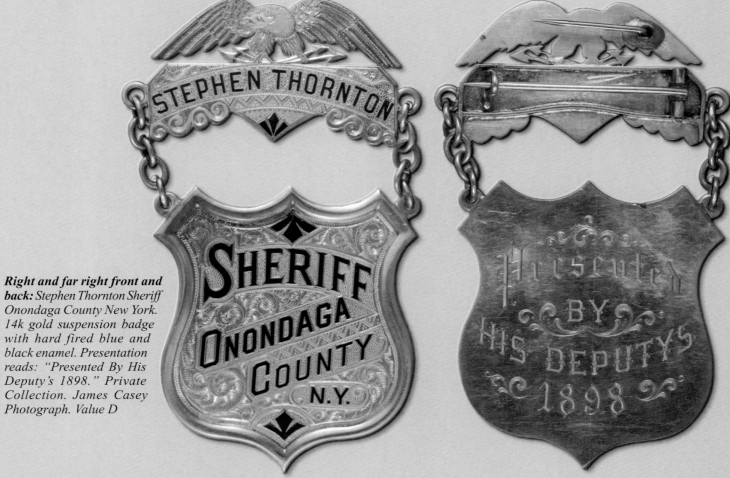

Right and far right front and back: Stephen Thornton Sheriff Onondaga County New York. 14k gold suspension badge with hard fired blue and black enamel. Presentation reads: "Presented By His Deputy's 1898." Private Collection. James Casey Photograph. Value D

105

NEW YORK

Above: Police Commissioner City Of Mt. Vernon. 14k gold adorned with diamonds. Presentation reads: "Presented To A.M. Anderson Deputy Com. Of Public Safety By His Friends FEB. 5, 1936." Private Collection. James Casey Photograph. Value D

Above: Sheriff Ontario County, New York. 14k gold. Obverse: "Geo L. Van Voorhis Bastian Bros. Gold." Private Collection. James Casey Photograph. Value D

Above: City of New York Deputy Chief. 14k gold with reverse hard fired blue enamel. Private Collection. James Casey Photograph. Value D

Right: New York City Metropolitan Police, Detective, circa 1870-1875, sterling silver with hard fired blue enamel. James Casey Collection. Value D

Right: New York City, 1st Issue, Surgeon, 14k gold, made by Chas. G. Braxmar Company, circa 1880. Ernie Leves Collection. Value C

Left: Troy, New York Police, 1st Issue, circa 1860. Ernie Leves Collection. Value A

106

Left: *David Holdsworth Constable Queens County New York. Stunning 14k gold eagle top shield, 3½" tall, adorned with diamonds, hard fired blue enamel. Presentation reads: "Presented By Neighbors And Friends May 15 1897." Private Collection. James Casey Photograph. Value D*

Above: *New York City Police Detective, Badge #1, 1880's. Value C*

Above: *Special Police 17 Utica New York - A silver color round badge with 6 point star in center, circa 1890-1920. Cut out numbers in the center. A unique and rare badge of yesteryear. No Hallmark. Photograph by Godfrey Digiorgi. Al Mize Collection. Value A*

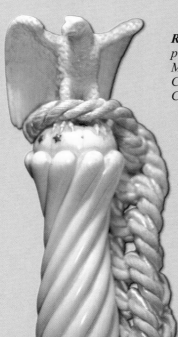

Right: *Daguerreotype photo image of a Metropolitan New York City police officer. James Casey Collection.*

Left: Benjamin Rosenthal Special Deputy Sheriff New York County New York. 14k gold with reverse hard fired enamel. Private Collection. James Casey Photograph. Value C

Above: Superintendent Fire and Police Telegraph Rochester New York. Superb 14k gold eagle top shield. Private Collection. James Casey Photograph. Value D

Above: Port Jervis, New York Police, circa 1890. Ernie Leves Collection. Value A

Right: Brooklyn, New York Municipal police officer image by the U.S. Portrait Company. James Casey Collection.

Above: Famous New York Police Captain "Clubber" Williams. James Casey Collection.

Left: This Brooklyn, New York police chief posed at the Silkworth studio for this cabinet card image. James Casey Collection.

Above: Second issue Metropolitan New York Police Department badge #1796, circa 1857-1870. James Casey Collection. Value C

Above: Alexander C. Dewar Sheriff Rensselaer County. 14k gold with hard fired blue enamel. Presentation reads: "To Alex C. Dewar From Troy Kiwanis Club Jan 1st 1937 14k." Private Collection. James Casey Photograph. Value D

Left: New York City police officer wearing a 5th issue badge, referred to as the "Potsy." Robinson & Roe Photo Studio. James Casey Collection.

NORTH CAROLINA

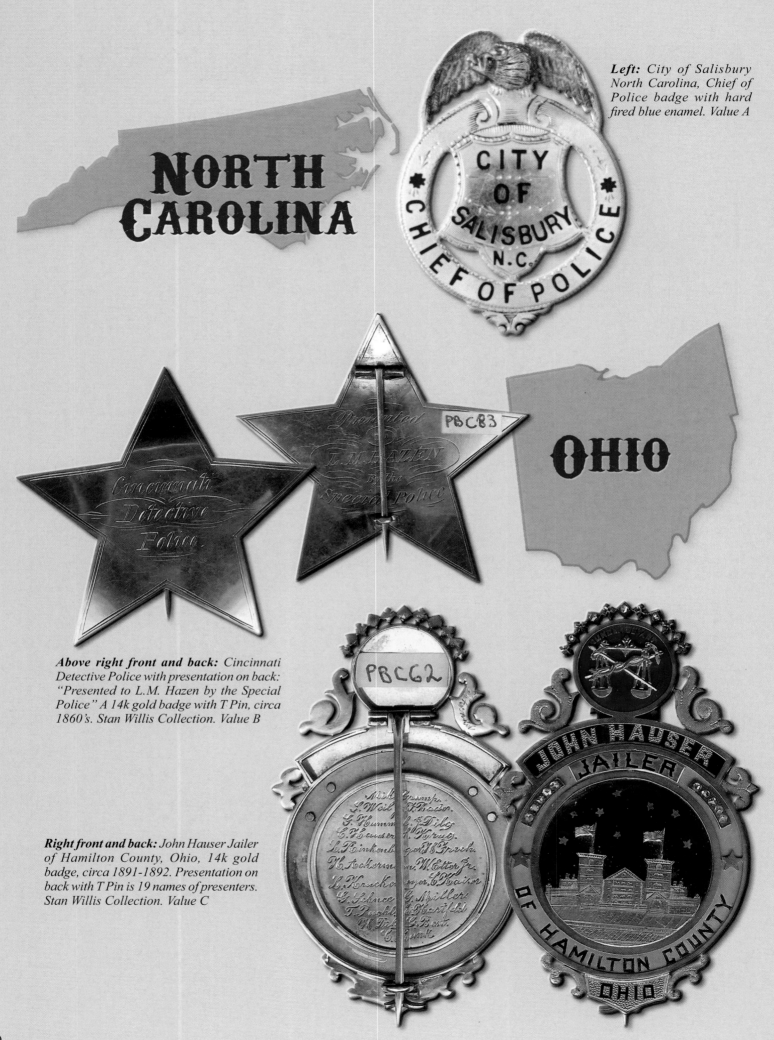

Left: *City of Salisbury North Carolina, Chief of Police badge with hard fired blue enamel. Value A*

OHIO

Above right front and back: *Cincinnati Detective Police with presentation on back: "Presented to L.M. Hazen by the Special Police" A 14k gold badge with T Pin, circa 1860's. Stan Willis Collection. Value B*

Right front and back: *John Hauser Jailer of Hamilton County, Ohio, 14k gold badge, circa 1891-1892. Presentation on back with T Pin is 19 names of presenters. Stan Willis Collection. Value C*

110

Above front and back: 18th Ward City of Cincinnati Councilman. Back presentation: "Presented to E. Hart by his many friends April, 1887." Stan Willis Collection

Above: Cincinnati, Ohio police officer. James Casey Collection.

Above front and back: Cincinnati Council 23rd Ward with back presentation: "Presented to Chas. A Freund from his Chase Club Friends Nov. 2, 1915." Stan Willis Collection. Value B

Above: Toledo Police. Silver and brass shield, circa 1870, T-pin. James Casey Collection. Value B

Left: Deputy Sheriff A.H. Short Lucas County, Ohio - A silver color circle with applied gold color state shaped shield in center of the badge. Hard fired blue enamel lettering and engraved by a master craftsman of yesteryear. This badge was issued and used by Mr. Short in 1923. A true beauty. Gold filled & STERLING. No Hallmark. Photograph by Godfrey Gigiorgi. Al Mize Collection. Value B

Right front and back: Charles A. Palmer, C.B. Wing, Cincinnati Police Department, 1898, Medal. Made by Frank Herschede (Jewelers) Cincinnati. Stan Willis Collection. Value B

Above: Inspector Of Detectives Toledo Louis J. Haas. Presentation reads: "Presented By Police Department And Friends Feb. 3 1923 The Roulet Co. Toledo O 14k gold. Private Collection. James Casey Photograph. Value D

Above: Village Marshal Norwood, Ohio. Back presentation: "Presented to Gerald Kehoe by his friends, August 6th, 1888." Stan Willis Collection. Value B

Above: Toledo O Asst Sup't Police Dep't Paul T. Fakehany. Presentation reads: "Presented July 31 1918 By His Syrian Friends 14k Gold. Private Collection. James Casey Photograph. Value D

Left: *Buck Garrett Chief Of Police Ardmore I.T. 14k gold suspension badge from Ardmore Indian Territory. James Casey Collection. Value E*

BUCK GARRETT

CHIEF OF POLICE ARDMORE I.T.

OKLAHOMA

OKLAHOMA CITY 579 POLICE

Above: *Sheriff of Carter County, Oklahoma, Buck Garrett and Deputy Bud Ballew. James Casey Collection.*

Right: *Oklahoma City Police #579. A wild cat sits atop this third issue badge. Gary Provenzano Collection. Al Tukey Photograph. Value A*

Above: *Buck Garrett (center) in front of Carter County Courthouse. (l. to r.) Fred Williams, Mr. Byrd, Jake Williams, unknown, Buck Garrett, Massey, Bill Powers, Bishop, Horace Kendal. Photo by Webb. James Casey Photo Collection.*

Police Band, Portland, Ore.

Above: Portland 13 Lieutenant Police - A gold color circle cut out 5 point star with hard fired blue enamel lettering and embellished with hand engraving and hand chasing by master jeweler. A real beauty. On the reverse is engraved " TO: Ben Wade from the boys of his relief" 14K gold. No Hallmark. Photograph by Godfrey Gigiorgi. Al Mize Collection. Value C

Above: Vintage postcard of the Portland, Oregon police band. James Casey Collection.

Below left: Portland Police #1946 badge, a large 2¾" circle cut out star with ball tips. Chris Christopher Collection. Value A

OREGON

Above: Klamath Falls #301 Police Reserve badge, a large 2¾" circle cut out star with ball tips. Jennifer Casey Collection. Value A

Above: The Shanafelt artist studio captured this image of Cottage Grove, Oregon police officer #1. James Casey Collection.

Above: Portland, Oregon police officer wearing badge #282. Photo by Portland Studios. James Casey Collection.

114

PENNSYLVANIA

Right: Borough of Throop Police, this folded eight point star is the 1st issue, circa 1894 and is considered rare. James Casey Collection. Value C

Right: Reading, Pennsylvania police patrol officer. Photo by the Strunk Studio. James Casey Collection.

Left: Harrisburg, Pennsylvania Police, circa 1875. Only two known to exist. Ernie Leves Collection. Value C

Above: Lawrence County Constable Taylor Township - A very unique and desirable badge made of silver. Note the star at the top resembles a crescent. Hard fired blue enamel lettering and hand engraved. A beauty! No Hallmark. Photograph by Godfrey Digiorgi. Al Mize Collection. Value A

Left: Easton, Pennsylvania cabinet photo of the police janitor. Palace Studio Photographer. James Casey Collection.

115

PENNSYLVANIA

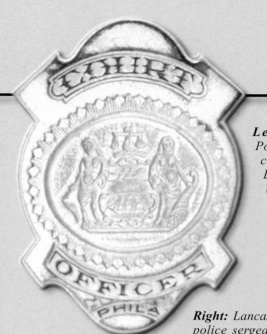

Left: Philadelphia Police, Court Officer, circa 1860's. Ernie Leves Collection. Value A

Right: Lancaster, Pennsylvania police sergeant. Photographer Black. James Casey Collection.

Above left: Chief Police Wilkesbarre. Beautiful shield, gold wash over nickel and hand chased, circa 1900. Doug Gist Collection. Value A

Above: Pittsburgh, Pennsylvania Police 1st Issue, circa 1850's. Ernie Leves Collection. Value C

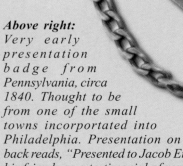

Above right: Very early presentation badge from Pennsylvania, circa 1840. Thought to be from one of the small towns incorporated into Philadelphia. Presentation on back reads, "Presented to Jacob Eriq by his friends as a testimonial of respect." James Casey Collection. Value E

117

RHODE ISLAND

Left: 1st issue New Port, Rhode Island, circa 1865. James Casey Collection. Value D

Above: Captain Providence Police, circa 1900. The seal displays the word "Whatcheer" the indigenous Indian greeting. James Casey Collection. Value A

Left: Bennettsville, South Carolina 3 Police. This large shield is made of nickel silver. James Casey Collection. Value A

SOUTH CAROLINA

SOUTH DAKOTA

Above front and back: Sioux Falls Police #12, shield cut out star design in nickel silver, circa 1900. James Casey Photograph. Value A

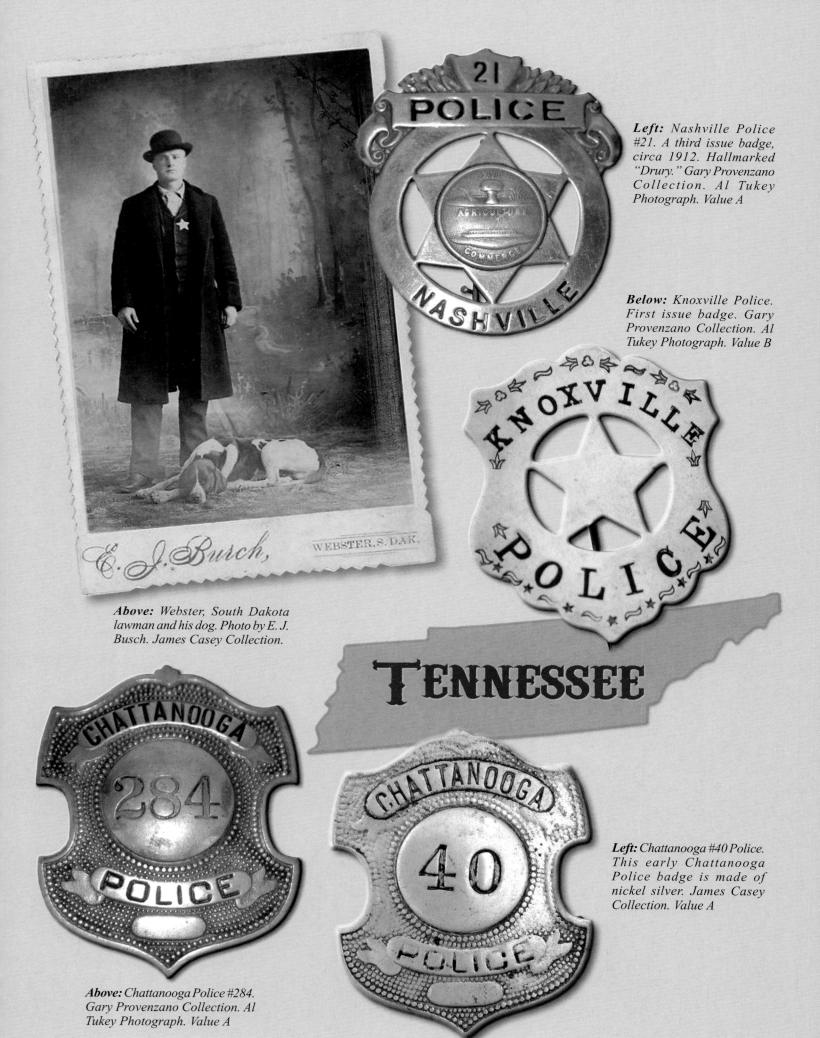

Left: *Nashville Police #21. A third issue badge, circa 1912. Hallmarked "Drury." Gary Provenzano Collection. Al Tukey Photograph. Value A*

Below: *Knoxville Police. First issue badge. Gary Provenzano Collection. Al Tukey Photograph. Value B*

Above: *Webster, South Dakota lawman and his dog. Photo by E. J. Busch. James Casey Collection.*

TENNESSEE

Left: *Chattanooga #40 Police. This early Chattanooga Police badge is made of nickel silver. James Casey Collection. Value A*

Above: *Chattanooga Police #284. Gary Provenzano Collection. Al Tukey Photograph. Value A*

119

TEXAS

Above: *Deputy Sheriff El Paso County. Circle star design in nickel silver, 1½", circa 1930. Value A*

Above: *Deputy Sheriff Bexar County, Texas, nickel silver, 1½" classic circle cut out star design. James Casey Photograph. Value A*

Right: *Beaumont, Texas, cabinet card photo of officer with tasseled baton and gauntlets in hand. James Casey Collection.*

120

Below right: Beaumont, Texas, cabinet card photo of a depot police officer. James Casey Collection.

Below right: City of San Antonio Motor Police # 4. Unique diamond style badge for traffic officers only, circa 1920. Gary Provenzano Collection. Al Tukey Photograph. Value A

Above: San Antonio Traffic Police #3. A shield badge with the Alamo sitting atop, circa 1930. Gary Provenzano Collection. Al Tukey Photograph. Value A

Above: The Chief of Police of Dallas, Texas, poses for this image. James Casey Collection.

121

Left: City Police #109 from San Antonio, Texas. A second issue, large nickel silver shield, circa 1890. Gary Provenzano Collection. Al Tukey Photograph. Value A

Above: Solid Gold badge of Elmo Strait, Chief Of Police Dallas. A beautifully designed suspension badge with hard fired blue enamel. James Casey Photo Collection. Value E

Above: Dallas, Texas, police officer cabinet card photo. James Casey Collection.

Above: Gold watch is inscribed "Captain Pat Garrett, Uvalde, Texas." Garrett, the slayer of Billy the Kid, was a Texas Ranger captain in 1884 and later was sheriff of Dona Ana County, New Mexico." John Boessenecker Collection.

UTAH

VIRGINIA

WASHINGTON

Above: *Tacoma, Washington, police badge #87, circle star design done in nickel silver. James Casey Photograph. Value A*

Above: *Battleground, Washington, cabinet card photo of officer Phil Gassoway wearing a suspension badge. Hoffsteater Studio Portland, Oregon. James Casey Collection.*

Above: *Captain Police Seattle. 14k gold, hard fired black enamel. Presentation reads: "A Token Of Highest Esteem To Walter R. Kirtley From Members Of The Seattle Police Dept. March 4, 1919–March 7, 1944 Service 14k." Private Collection. James Casey Photograph. Value D*

Above: *Deputy Game Warden Grays Harbor County, Washington, Badge. James Casey Photo Collection. Value A*

124

Above: Seattle Park Commissioner - A silver color shield with cut out star center. Hard fired blue enamel lettering and hand engraved and hand chased by a master craftsman. Used in the 1930's. Sterling - No Hallmark. Photograph by Godfrey Digiorgi. Al Mize Collection. Value B

Above: Port Townsend, Washington, police officer. James Casey Collection.

Above: Bellingham Police Motor Patrol #3 - Nice example of a motor patrol badge. Doug Gist Collection. Value A

Above: Everett #4 Police - Shield and cut out star design. Doug Gist Collection. Value A

Above: Deputy Game Warden Pierce County badge made of nickel. James Casey Photo Collection. Value A

U.S. FEDERAL

Above: Penal & Correctional Institutions # 119 - U. S. Officer - A gold color eagle top total custom die badge that resembles the old Potsy badge. Hard fired reverse blue enamel adorns this old and rare badge. A beauty to behold. Used up till 1930 when the Federal Bureau of Prisons started. Hallmarked: "N.C. Walter & Sons, NY." Photograph by James Casey. Al Mize Collection. Value C

Above: U.S. Customs Treasury Department Customs Agent #174, circa 1930. Al Mize Collection. Value B

Above: U.S. Customs Inspector 73 - A very unique and rare gold color shield badge. All raised lettering and applied numbers. Hallmark: "C. G. Braxmar - 10 Maiden Lane, NY." Photograph by Godfrey Digiorgi. Al Mize Collection. Value B

Right: DeputyUnited States Marshal Presentation on back reads: "Presented To George Whittell By Fred Esola United States Marshal Aug. 14, 1935 N.D.C. No. 8 Irvine & Jachens 14K." Private Collection. James Casey Photograph. Value D

Above: U.S. Customs Inspector - A gold color round badge with hard fired black enamel lettering and full custom design. Used in early 1920's. Hallmark: "C. G. Braxmar - 10 Maiden Lane -NY." Photograph by Godfrey Digiorgi. Al Mize Collection. Value B

126

Right: U.S. Department of the Interior Fish and Wildlife Service Alaska Enforcement Agent, circa 1920-1950, 10 k. gold filled. Al Mize Collection. Value B

Above: U.S. Department of the Interior Fish and Wildlife Service Bureau of Sport Fisheries & Wildlife, U.S. Deputy Game Warden, circa 1930-1960, made by Metal Arts. Al Mize Collection. Value C

Right: Deputy Special Officer US Indian Service 163 - A gold color eagle top shield with hard fired black enamel lettering and Indian Head center. Same head that was later used on the nickle. Issued to Prohibition Agents charged with enforcing laws on the reservations circa 1917-1932. Hallmark: "Robbins Co. Attleboro, Mass." Photograph by Godfrey Digiorgi. Al Mize Collection. Value C

Above: United States Shipping Board - A beautiful round badge with hard fired black enamel lettering. A custom ship in the center of the badge is magnificent. Used by inspectors during WW1 who were charged with purchasing war vessels, inspecting ships, auditing for fraud. A very rare and now defunct agency. Photograph by Godfrey Digiorgi. Hallmark: Whithead & Hoag - Newark, NJ Al Mize Collection. Value A

Above: US Marshal 14k gold with raised gold lettering. Obverse reads: "J. DYSON 14K." Private Collection. James Casey photo. Value D

Left: Deputy U.S. Marshal - A silver color 5 point star with soft black enamel lettering and an old saddle pin back. Used by Deputies during the latter 1880's of the west. No Hallmark. Photograph by Godfrey Digiorgi. Al Mize Collection. Value A

Right: Deputy US Marshal in reverse hard fired blue enamel on this 14k gold badge with enameled red white and blue stars and stripes design. Private Collection. James Casey Photograph. Value D

Left: Deputy U.S. Marshal S.D.O. - A silver color shield with soft black enamel lettering. Used in the Southern District of Ohio, circa 1880. Old saddle pin back. Hallmark: "Jas. Murdock & Co, 165 Race Street." Photograph by Godfrey Digiorgi. Al Mize Collection. Value B

Right: Inspector Canal Zone Customs - A beautiful custom die badge with hard fired black enamel lettering and a ship with sails entering the canal zone from open water. Gold Filled. No Hallmark. Photograph by Godfrey Digiorgi. Al Mize Collection. Value B

Above: United States Government Guard Div. of Suburban Resettlement Resettlement Administration 56 - A very early badge from World War II issued to those federal officers charged with guarding property and personnel in the resettlement act. There is no Hallmark. Photograph by Godfrey Digiorgi. Al Mize Collection. Value A

Left: Inspector U.S. Customs Philadelphia 68 - A gold color eagle top shield with hard fired blue enamel lettering. A beauty with a customs seal attached to back of badge. Hallmark: "Diegas & Clust - NY." Photograph by Godfrey Digiorgi. Al Mize Collection. Value B

Above: A rare image of a old west U. S. Marshal's office. James Casey Collection.

Above: Alva McDonald United States Marshal. Presentation reads: "Presented By Kelly McRoach Charles Derr 1922 14k." Private Collection. James Casey Photograph. Value D

Above: US Prohibition Service Treasury Department - Gold color custom die badge with hard fired blue reverse enameling. A custom eagle in the center of the die. First issue of the newly formed Prohibition Service. This is the same badge style that was issued to Elliot Ness. A historic beauty. Hallmark: "Bastian Bros. Rochester, NY." Photograph by Godfrey Digiorgi. Al Mize Collection. Value C

Above: U.S. Marshal Eastern District Michigan. 14k gold. Presentation reads: "Henry Behrendt From Citizen Friends In Commendation Of Efficient And Loyal Services As Chief Of Police Lansing Michigan, 1914. Private Collection. James Casey Photograph. Value D

129

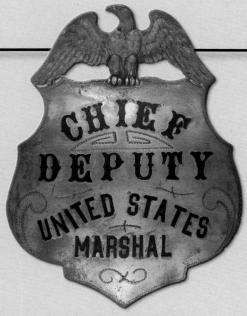

Left: U.S. Inspector Steam Vessels 278 - A magnificent silver shield, with hand engraving throughout the badge depicting a steam vessel on the ocean waters. A beautiful, rare and historic badge from 1880-1910 era. T pin back. No Hallmark. Photograph by Godfrey Digiorgi. Al Mize Collection Value C

Above: Chief Deputy United States Marshal. Sterling silver with hard fired enamel and hand chasing. Private Collection. James Casey Photograph. Value D

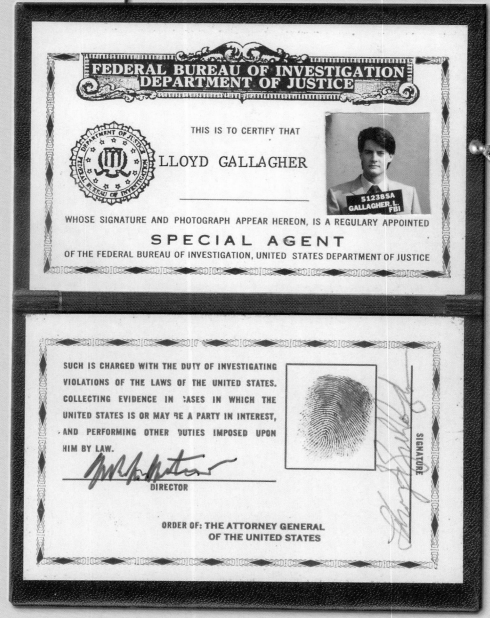

Above: United States Marshal. 14k gold 5 point star adorned with the American eagle with US in chest. Presentation reads: "Dewey C. Bailey June 1898 14k. Private Collection. James Casey Photograph. Value D

Left: Movie prop FBI credential for the 1987 movie "The Hidden" starring Kyle MacLachlan pictured on the credential. James Casey Collection.

130

Left: U.S. Indian Forest Service Department of the Interior - A beautiful silver color shield with double pin back. Used by Indian Forest Service in era of 1890-1920. A true beauty and very historical for Indian Service collectors. No Hallmark. Photograph by Godfrey Digiorgi. Al Mize Collection. Value C

Right: United States Marshal Supreme Court J.M. Wright "In Appreciation 21 Yrs. Devoted Service Jan 4 1888 – Jan 4, 1909 From Melville W. Fuller – John M. Harlan – James H. Mckenney – Tiffanny & Co. 18k." Private Collection. James Casey Photograph. Value D

Above: United States Marshal, No. Dist. Cal. Beautiful layered 14k gold 3" badge, with hard fired blue enamel, red white and blue enameled stars and stripes center seal. Made by Ed Jones Company, Oakland, California. Private Collection. James Casey Photograph. Value E

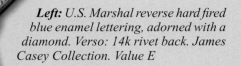

Left: Inspector U.S. Public Health Service 144 - A very old and rare silver color shield with soft black enamel lettering, circa 1890-1900. Saddle pin back. Hallmark: "Lamb Stencil and Seal, Wash, DC." Photograph by Godfrey Digiorgi. Al Mize Collection. Value A

Left: U.S. Marshal reverse hard fired blue enamel lettering, adorned with a diamond. Verso: 14k rivet back. James Casey Collection. Value E

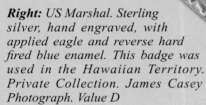

Right: U.S.R.R. Administration of America Police K.C. Terminal R.R. 48 - A silver color 6 point folded star with soft black enamel lettering. The gold color heart "of America" in the center. A very rare old railroad badge that speaks for itself. Have the original letter from the Superintendant stating this badge was last used in the 1920's. Saddle pin back. Hallmarked: "Allen Stamp & Seal, Kansas City." Photograph by Godfrey Gigiorgi. Al Mize Collection. Value B

Above: US Treasury Department Inspector Bureau of Industrial Alcohol - A beautiful gold color badge with white reverse enamel. Used in early days of Prohibition in accounting for industrial alcohol versus drinking alcohol, 1930 era. No Hallmark. Photograph by Godfrey Digiorgi. Al Mize Collection. Value C

Right: US Marshal. Sterling silver, hand engraved, with applied eagle and reverse hard fired blue enamel. This badge was used in the Hawaiian Territory. Private Collection. James Casey Photograph. Value D

Above: War Department US Military Intelligence - A beautiful oval shield with hard fired reverse blue enamel lettering and an intertwined US in the center. A very rare badge from World War I. Sterling - No Hallmark. Photograph by Godfrey Digiorgi. Al Mize Collection. Value C

Right: US Deputy Marshal. Sterling silver, with applied eagle and reverse hard fired blue enamel. This badge was used in the Hawaiian Territory. Private Collection. James Casey Photograph. Value D

INDEX

BADGES

BADGES ARE INDEXED ACCORDING TO TEXT ON FRONT OF BADGE — TOP TO BOTTOM — LEFT TO RIGHT.

Left: Photographer W. L. Cover captures this image of a Baltimore, Maryland lawman. James Casey collection.

134

Above: Famed San Francisco badge maker J. C. Irvine made this sterling silver and gold washed star, circa 1886 while he was at 339 Kearny Street. Across the hallway competitors Wirth & Jachens were manufacturing badges as well. The great San Francisco earthquake of 1906 destroyed the building of all three men. Starting over was an expensive venture and the three craftsmen joined forces and established the Irvine Wirth & Jachens Company. James Casey Collection. Value C

Above: New York city policeman by Photographer R. Stollmack Brooklyn, New York. James Casey Collection.

• Police Department City of New York Sergeant	103
• Police Dept City of N. Y. Hostler #18	104
• Police Detective #7 Stockton	52
• Police Detective New York City #1	107
• Police Humboldt, Nebr.	89
• Police Los Gatos Officer	59
• Policeman Farmersville Police #1	66
• Policeman San Bernardino Police #16	44
• Police No. 1 Pueblo	70
• Police Patrolman #7 Huntington Park	22
• Police Pompton Lakes New Jersey Sergeant	94
• Police State of New Hampshire Conway N.H. #8	91
• Police Yuma Arizona	6
• Policewoman Santa Monica Police Record Bureau	24
• Pomona Park #1 Police	27
• Portland #13 Lieutenant Police	114
• Portland #1946 Police	114
• Property Clerk #124 Police Sacramento	40
• Railroad And Steamboat Police #696 California Southern Pacific Co.	69
• "R. D. Carter" G. R. 1882 1927 Sheriff Of Nevada County	35
• Red Bluff Police	65
• "Reno Bartolomie" Sheriff Mendocino County	29
• Retired San Francisco #A87 Police	50
• "R. L. Marr Jr." Under Sheriff Lake County	21
• Roundsman Precinct #28 Brooklyn Police	96
• Roundsman Richmond Co. Police #2	102
• Sacramento #46 Police	40
• Sacramento #90 Police	40
• Sacramento #419 Police	41
• Salt Lake City Police	123
• "Sam Ryan" Riverside County Sheriff	39
• San Antonio Traffic #3 Police	121
• San Francisco #6 Police Honorary	46
• San Francisco #793 Police USA	50
• San Rafael Constable Township	28
• Sausalito #6 Police	3
• Seattle Park Commissioner	125
• Secretary Los Angeles Police To Chief	26
• Secretary Police Sacramento	43
• Sergeant #4 Police	42
• Sergeant #82 Police	51
• Sergeant #94 Police	43
• Sergeant #244 Police	14
• Sergeant #281 Police	43
• Sergeant #677 S.F. Police	52
• Sergeant #3138 S.F. Police Reserve	50
• Sergeant Of Police #13 Sacramento	1
• Sergeant Police City of New Orleans	80
• Sheriff	87
• Sheriff "B. F. Walker" Siskiyou Co.	62
• Sheriff Cal Nevada County	16
• Sheriff Del Norte County "Austin "Bud" Huffman"	16
• Sheriff Hudson County N.J.	94
• Sheriff Humboldt Co. Iowa	78
• Sheriff Humboldt Co. Nev	90
• Sheriff Lake County Indiana	77
• Sheriff Modoc County	16
• Sheriff of Hawaii	73
• Sheriff of Marion Co.	77
• Sheriff of Oahu	73
• Sheriff of Sangamon Co.	75
• Sheriff Ontario Co. N.Y.	106
• Sheriff Sac. County Cal.	42
• Sheriff Sacramento Co. Calif.	42
• Sheriff Santa Clara County	59
• Sheriff Sonoma Co. Cal.	63
• Sheriff Sonoma, Co. Calif.	63
• Sheriff Tehama Co.	65
• Sheriff's Sergeant Santa Clara Co. #93	56
• Sierra Sheriff County	60
• Sioux Falls #12 Police	118
• So. Danvers Police	82
• Solano County Sheriff's Air Sq. Deputy #1F8	63

• Special Police #17 Utica N.Y.	107
• "Stanley Fine" Sheriff Eureka County, Nev.	90
• State Humane Officer of California #2	69
• State of California Railroad Police Southern Pacific Co. #76 Steamboat Police	69
• State of Nebraska G. F. & P. Commission #4	89
• State Road Commission Police	123
• "Stephen Thornton" Sheriff Onondaga County N.Y.	105
• St. Paul #14 Police	85
• Street Sergeant 23rd District	116
• Superintendent Fire And Police Telegraph Rochester N.Y.	108
• Superintendent Juvenile Department Police Sacramento	43
• Surgeon Police Department City of New York	106
• Territory of Alaska Highway Patrol #37	6
• "T.M. Brown" Sheriff Humboldt Co.	19
• Toledo O. Bureau of IAR Ass't. Sup't. Police Dept. "Paul T. Fakehany"	112
• Toledo Police	111
• Traffic Captain County of Hawaii T.H. Police	73
• Traffic San Mateo Co. #4	53
• Troy Police Force #23	106
• Ukiah #1 Police	29
• Under Sheriff Butte Co., Calif.	13
• Under Sheriff Del Norte County	16
• Under Sheriff Hudson County N.J.	94
• Under Sheriff Modoc County	31
• Under Sheriff Napa County	32
• Under Sheriff Santa Barbara County Cal.	54
• Under Sheriff Santa Clara Co.	58
• Under Sheriff Tehama Co.	65
• United States Government Guard Div. of Suburban Resettlement Resettlement Administration #56	128
• United States Marshal	130
• United States Marshal No. Dist. Cal.	131

• United States Marshal Supreme Court "J.M. Wright"	131
• United States Shipping Board #880	127
• U.S. Customs Inspector	126
• U.S. Customs Inspector #73	126
• U.S. Customs Treasury Department Customs Agent #174	126
• U.S. Department of the Interior Fish and Wildlife Service Alaska Enforcement Agent	127
• U.S. Department of the Interior Fish and Wildlife Service Bur. of Sport Fisheries & Wildlife U.S. Deputy Game Warden	127
• U.S. Deputy Marshal	132
• U.S. Indian Forest Service Dept. of the Interior	131
• U.S. Inspector Steam Vessels #278	130
• U.S. Marshal	127, 131, 132
• U.S. Marshal Eastern District Michigan	129
• U.S. Prohibition Service Treasury Department	129
• U.S.R.R. Administration Of America Police K.C. Terminal R.R. #48	132
• US Treasury Department Inspector Bureau of Industrial Alcohol	132
• Venice #1 Police	25
• Village Marshal Norwood	112
• War Department US Military Intelligence	132
• "W. C. Abernethy, Jr." Under-Sheriff Plumas County Cal	38
• "W. E. Colburn" Calif. Deputy Sheriff Riverside County	39
• Westfield Police	93
• West Hoboken Police Det. Lieut.	94
• Wichita Police #68	79
• "Wm. Fonseca" Constable Placer Co.	38
• "Wm H. Craig" Sheriff Monroe Co. N.Y.	101
• "Wm. Pederson" Sheriff Humboldt County California	19
• "Wm W. Arnett" City & County of Denver Chief Sheriff Deputy	71

NAMES